The EVERYTHING
Guide to Writing Research I

D1469948

Dear Reader:

Is this your first research paper? I can clearly remember the first research paper I worked on. I had no idea that I was supposed to be doing anything different than I had done for previous reports, so I sailed through and eventually handed in what I thought was a wonderful paper. Then it was graded and I got a C. What a shock! If I had done some background reading, or if I had really been paying attention to what my instructor was saying, I might have realized that there is much more to it. I've forgotten the topic of that paper, but I will always remember getting that big red C when I thought deserved an A.

Maybe you're in the same circumstance. Maybe you've already done one or more research papers but you seem to be missing something. The grades on your papers are never as high as you are capable of getting. If that's the case, this book is for you. Whether you read through all of it or just the parts that answer your specific questions, you'll be able to fill in the missing pieces in your next research paper—and maybe earn that A!

Cathy Spalding

The EVERYTHING® Series

Editorial

Publishing Director	Gary M. Krebs
Associate Managing Editor	Laura M. Daly
Copy Chief	Brett Palana-Shanahan
Acquisitions Editor	Gina Chaimanis
Development Editor	Luann Rouff
Production Editor	Casey Ebert

Production

Director of Manufacturing & Technology	Susan Beale
Associate Director of Production	Michelle Roy Kelly
Series Designers	Daria Perreault
	Colleen Cunningham
	John Paulhus
Cover Design	Paul Beatrice
	Matt LeBlanc
Layout and Graphics	Colleen Cunningham
	Holly Curtis
	Erin Dawson
	Sorae Lee
Series Cover Artist	Barry Littmann

Visit the entire Everything® Series at *www.everything.com*

THE

EVERYTHING®

GUIDE TO
WRITING
RESEARCH PAPERS

Ace your next project with
step-by-step expert advice!

Cathy Spalding

Adams Media
Avon, Massachusetts

To Mom and Dad, for teaching me to follow my dreams.

An Everything® Series Book.
Everything® and everything.com® are registered trademarks of F+W Publications, Inc.

Published by Adams Media, an F+W Publications Company
57 Littlefield Street, Avon, MA 02322 U.S.A.
www.adamsmedia.com

ISBN: 1-59337-422-4
Printed in the United States of America.

J I H G F E D C B A

Library of Congress Cataloging-in-Publication Data
Spalding, Cathy.
The everything guide to writing research papers / Cathy Spalding.
p. cm. -- (An everything series book)
Includes bibliographical references.
1. Report writing--Handbooks, manuals, etc. 2. Research--Hand-
books, manuals, etc. I. Title. II. Series: Everything series.
LB2369.S6295 2005
371.3'028'1--dc22
2005015481

This book is available at quantity discounts for bulk purchases.
For information, please call 1-800-872-5627.

Contents

Acknowledgments

Writing a book at first appears to be a solitary pursuit, but there is a whole group of people behind this project. Without their encouragement, support, and information, this book would not be possible. To Trevor, Tanner, Miranda, Alanna, and Heather for "holding down the fort" while I was otherwise occupied. To Pat and Mike for the football game diversion, and to Denise and June each for their morning with the munchkin.

The many people who patiently answered questions and offered suggestions have been a huge help to me. Specifically, to Wendy for helping me understand what goes on behind a library desk. To Ann Riedling for sending professional advice on plagiarism and Web site evaluation. And finally to Barb, my agent, and Gina, my editor, for giving me the opportunity to write this, answering my questions whenever I asked, giving me constructive feedback, and offering encouragement. You had confidence in my abilities even when I had doubts, and I am grateful for that. The guidance you offered in walking me through the process of writing this, my first book, was beyond the call of duty.

Top Ten Research Paper Topics

1. Attention Deficit Disorder—Is Attention Deficit Disorder overdiagnosed today? Is it just an excuse for poor parenting and a way to get unnecessary drugs, or is there a real crisis?

2. College Students and Credit Cards—Why do so many credit card companies market to college students? Do students really have a need for credit when they don't generally have an income?

3. Drugs and Athletes—How strong is the pressure on athletes to use performance-enhancing drugs? Is the problem better or worse than commonly thought?

4. Eating Disorders—What causes eating disorders in teens? Is anyone ever really cured for good?

5. High-School Dropouts—Which famous people were high-school dropouts? Are there the same career opportunities for dropouts nowadays?

6. Global Warming—Is global warming caused by humans, or is it part of a natural cycle of events? Is everything being done that can be done to slow global warming?

7. Identity Theft—How do thieves go about stealing someone else's identity? What can happen to you if someone steals yours?

8. Rising College Tuition—How do college tuitions today compare with those in the past? What is the forecast for tuition increases?

9. Students Cheating—How many students cheat on tests and assignments? Is the problem getting worse?

10. Vehicles Powered by Electricity—What are the limitations of electric-powered vehicles? Will this technology evolve enough to take over from gas-powered vehicles?

Introduction

▶ WHEN YOU ARE FIRST ASSIGNED a research paper, you will probably have one of two reactions. On the one hand, you might dread the whole process, feel overwhelmed, or turn into a nervous wreck. On the other hand, you might be excited, looking forward to the opportunity to fully explore a topic that really appeals to you. If you react the second way, you are ready to get started. You already have the positive attitude that will help you achieve your goals. If you react the first way, you'll need to take another look at the situation. You are capable of completing this assignment, and with some guidance along the way you can stop fearing the process and instead work your way through it step by step. As you progress, you just might find yourself enjoying the challenge.

A research paper can be a very intriguing project. You are usually given at least partial freedom to select your own topic. Therefore, you can pick something that you find personally fascinating. You can conduct research on a topic that you feel strongly about or that you have a desire to learn more about. And you will learn much, much more about it than you otherwise would. Because you will collect research from such a wide variety of sources, and then compare and analyze it using your own opinions and ideas, you will gain a mastery of your topic. Instead of the paper being a dull and boring report on a topic that doesn't interest you, you'll be inspired to write an interesting and fun paper because you really care about the topic.

This book guides you through every phase of the project and explains in detail how to accomplish each task. If you don't know how to get started or what to do along the way, you can simply follow the sequence of steps. Those of you who have some experience with research projects can just go to the section or chapter that pertains to your needs.

As you read through this book, you will learn exactly what a research paper involves, how to choose a suitable topic, and how to schedule your time so that you complete the paper by the due date without a last-minute panic. You will learn how to make full use of all research sources, including traditional reference materials, the Internet, films, television, radio, music recordings, museums, and government institutions. After that you will find out how to conduct an interview, and with whom. You will learn how to take good notes and how to format your research sources for the bibliography. You will learn how to prepare an outline and how to organize your notes into the best order for writing the draft versions of your paper. You will find out how to check your facts, spelling, and grammar, and ensure well-crafted writing. You will be shown which graphic elements could be included in your paper to improve its value. You then will learn how to produce your final draft of the research paper, how to present it orally, and how to publish it. The last chapter discusses the new skills you acquired through this process, and other ways in which you can apply them.

Chapter 1

Research Paper Basics

Throughout school you have had to write reports, including numerous book reports, reports about countries, and reports about important historical people and events. Now it is time to use all of those research skills and much, much more to produce your own research paper. Although it may be intimidating at first, this is an opportunity to totally immerse yourself in a subject that interests you. Writing a research paper is a project that enables you to learn more about a topic than the average person typically knows.

What a Research Paper Is and Is Not

Many people have only a vague idea of what a research paper is. They know it involves research, so material about a specific topic needs to be gathered. They also know it is a paper, which is a written assignment involving a significant amount of homework. If the thought of writing your research paper makes you cringe, it might help to clarify your understanding of what a research paper is (and isn't).

What It Is

A research paper is an in-depth study of a specific and distinct topic. It includes not only factual research from a wide variety of sources, but also the writer's interpretation of that research. This interpretation is a key element of the true research paper.

Make sure you fully understand what is expected in your paper before you begin your research, because each instructor has certain expectations. On the one hand, you don't want to waste your time going into more detail than is needed. On the other hand, you don't want to complete your paper only to find that you neglected to include everything that is required.

Writing a research paper gives you a chance to debunk popular myths or convince others to consider new and different ways of looking at an issue. However, you must be careful to back up your perspective with facts that show how you reached your conclusions.

Though a research paper covers the topic in question completely, it is centered on a specific and distinct topic as opposed to a general one. Suppose that you want to write a paper about dogs. "Dogs" by itself is a very general topic and much too broad to cover completely. A better topic for a research paper might be to explore how proper exercise and nutrition contribute to a dog's longevity.

What It Is Not

A research paper is not just a factual report, although facts are a part of the paper. Nor is it an editorial, or simply an expression of the writer's opinions, although that too is part of the paper. A simple collection of information does not constitute a research paper. It is the personal perspective that distinguishes a research paper from any other type of report.

How Research Papers Differ from Reports

All those reports you wrote in the past gave you an excellent background in researching facts, but now you understand that a research paper is much more than a collection of facts. Unlike a report, a research paper does not just describe something. It compares, persuades, or analyzes. To fully understand what a research paper is, you need to know how it differs from a regular report.

ALERT!

Take care not to choose a topic that is too narrow in focus. If you do, you will discover that not enough information is available, and what information there is will be hard to find. Although you can often supplement the available information by conducting numerous interviews or doing surveys, be aware that these all take time.

To begin with, a research paper has a much narrower focus than does a report. While a report might describe a particular country in general terms, a research paper delves deeper, discussing how the people of that country are preserving their customs or language, or whether the natural resources of that country should be exported. This narrower focus means that, as the researcher, you go deeper into the topic. Rather than simply finding and presenting facts, you develop a fuller understanding of your topic and an informed opinion about the issues involved.

Including Your Own Thoughts and Opinions

What makes a research paper truly unique to you is that it includes your own thoughts, perceptions, and ideas about your topic. In some papers, you form an opinion through your research. In other cases, you may change your opinion during the course of your research. If you are writing a persuasive paper, you try to convince others to agree with that opinion. For analytical papers, you make comparisons between your interpretations and the facts.

Question the Facts

As you gather material, you must question the facts, dissecting each and every piece of information to discern whether it is true and reliable. Obviously, some facts are straightforward. Suppose your paper is titled "Does Requiring School Uniforms Reduce Incidents of Bullying?" You uncover the facts that a particular school of 800 students had forty reported cases of bullying in one school year. After uniforms became mandatory, the number of reported cases of bullying dropped to thirty-two cases. The number of students is a fact, as is the number of reported cases of bullying. But when working on a research paper, you must question all aspects of the data. How many people do the reported cases of bullying involve? Were there repeat offenders (and victims)? Did some of those students involved leave the school once uniforms were required? What is the process for reporting bullying? Have any changes been made to this process? Once you start to question the facts, you begin to realize how to approach this important aspect of your research paper and let your own unique voice shine through.

QUESTION?

Will I be able to do all my research in the school library?
Probably not, although much of the information is available there, particularly if your library offers Internet access. Some of it won't be, and you'll uncover the rest of the information by conducting personal interviews and visiting museums or other historical sites.

Use Many Sources

When you last wrote a report, you quite possibly used an encyclopedia, surfed the Internet for further information, and maybe found an additional book or two to round it out. You will use those same sources for your research paper, but you will also use many more. Your research will include checking trade journals, visiting historical places of interest, and even conducting interviews. While this may sound like a lot of work, you are simply going to where the information is. In order to truly dig into a topic, you need as much information as possible, and from as wide a realm as possible. Using the many other sources available opens up the topic to you and ultimately makes the final paper easier to write. Once you gather all the information you can find from every possible source, the information will be easier to interpret. Because you have such a wide range of information and such detailed data, you will find that it all fits together logically.

Critical Thinking Skills

Instructors assign research papers for a good reason, even if that reason isn't readily apparent to you right now. Not only will you learn how to research a topic in depth and use resources that you have previously left unexplored; the new skills you learn or develop from writing your paper also will serve you throughout school and in the workplace, because the project will nurture your critical thinking abilities.

FACT

Typical major research papers are twenty pages long, typed, double-spaced, and one-sided. However, a recent study of secondary school history teachers revealed that many don't assign papers beyond about eight pages in length because they don't have the time to mark them properly.

"Critical thinking" is one of those catchy phrases educators are fond of using. What it really means is the process of gathering information and then dissecting and analyzing and evaluating it to arrive at your own conclusions. Not only is this important in future schooling; it is a key life skill.

Unfortunately, it is not something you can learn at one sitting. Critical thinking skills must be practiced, and a research paper is an ideal vehicle for developing these skills.

Fully Understand Your Topic

Research projects are assigned to ensure that you learn your topic inside and out. You can't possibly write a research paper about a topic with which you are only halfway familiar. You need to dig up every piece of information you can find on your topic. You have to learn your topic in depth. By the time you are finished, you will be the class expert on that subject.

Obviously, you cannot cut corners and still write a good research paper. Nor can you copy from someone else or delegate some of the work to another student, because you would not both have the same views. The only way to be successful on a project of this scope is to put a full effort into the entire project so that you end up fully understanding everything you researched. This type of research work tends to remain with you. Years later, you may still be able to vividly recall parts of a research paper, whereas dry facts from an ordinary report are long forgotten.

Think Independently

Because your paper must include your own perspective on a particular topic, thoroughly researching the available information about that subject enables you to sort out your personal feelings about it. The degree to which you express those opinions in your paper depends on the type of paper you are writing. You also have to decide what you think is believable and what should be questioned. It is up to you to determine how you think one event has affected another, and whether that effect has been negative or positive. You cannot completely form your view until you have done all the research yourself. The opinions you form show that you can think independently and that you can analyze all aspects of a situation to arrive at your own conclusions.

Communicate Clearly

It is not enough just to research facts and form your own opinions; you also must learn how to communicate clearly to the reader. Your thoughts must be organized, and the paper must flow from one section to the next. Whereas in the past you have presented facts, now you will combine those facts with your own analysis. Your efforts should result in a research paper that is free of errors and interesting to read, leaving the reader with a clear understanding of what the paper is about and where you stand on the issues it raises.

Analytical Research Papers

One of two main types of research papers, an analytical paper closely scrutinizes, or examines, a given topic. Although it still involves critical thinking skills, the analytical research paper differs from the general research paper described in the previous section.

Maintaining Neutrality

When you write an analytical research paper, you remain neutral. Although you may develop a feeling for one position or the other, your paper never shows this. You avoid defining anything as better or safer or more important. You present all aspects of your topic, but do not show whether you agree or disagree with them. Suppose your paper is on "The Effect of Part-Time Jobs on a Student's Education." You could discuss both the benefits of holding a part-time job (job experience, unique skills learned) and the drawbacks (incomplete homework, tired students), but at no time would you say whether students should or should not have part-time jobs.

It can be difficult to remain neutral, especially as your research progresses. If you find this to be the case, consider switching to a persuasive research paper. Of course, this is only an option if your instructor has indicated that a persuasive paper is acceptable.

Historical and Current Events

An analytical research paper can examine the effect of an event on other events. The events can be in the past, present, or future. For example, you can do a "what if" exercise: imagine how things would be different if President John F. Kennedy hadn't been assassinated, or if women around the world had never been allowed to have more than one baby. Each event that occurs sets off a chain of other events. If your paper is centered on an event or a person, you can talk about how that event or that person's actions changed history. What would be different if that event hadn't happened at all? What effects are we still going to feel years from now? How have that person's actions (or inventions, or lack of action) affected our lives?

Pick Out Key Issues

An important part of the analytical research paper is determining the key issue or issues. In some cases these are easy to find, but in others you may have to look a little harder. You don't want to miss a glaringly obvious point, which is why you will do extensive research. If you gather sufficient information, you will be able to choose the main points to analyze further.

Persuasive Research Papers

When you write a persuasive research paper, you attempt to persuade the reader to agree with you. This is an ideal type of research paper for those of you who like to debate.

Take a Position

In a persuasive research paper, you take a stand either for or against an idea or an issue. Usually you begin the paper by stating your position. This is commonly known as the *thesis statement*. Whole books have been written about how to write a thesis statement, but it doesn't have to be that difficult. Basically, it should sum up, usually in one sentence but occasionally in two, what your paper is about and what you are trying to prove. The conclusion of your paper is a restatement of your main thesis, showing how you have proven it. Your entire paper supports your position and and attempts to convince others that you are right. Be very clear about which side you take in a persuasive paper. Your purpose is not to look at both sides, as you would in an analytical paper, but to prove that your side is correct.

Gather Arguments from Others

The research you gather for a persuasive paper reinforces your stance on the issues. You will uncover supporting arguments from other people and events that support your position. You also will uncover arguments against your position, which are just as important as those that support it, because they help you to clarify and refine your position.

For example, if your chosen topic were "Are Commercial Trucks Making Our Highways Unsafe?" you might take the position that truckers are driving too fast and not getting enough sleep. You would gather statistics on accidents involving commercial trucks, read through government regulations regarding time spent driving, and interview truck drivers, police, and accident victims. Though the accident victims might support your position, it is unlikely that all, if any, of the truck drivers would. However, their opinions and arguments would become part of a well-rounded discussion.

ALERT!

In some cases, you may not be able to find others who agree with your position. Maybe you are the first person to openly question something, or the first to disagree with the status quo. If this happens, your own arguments must be very strong. You must uncover concrete evidence to back up your case.

Add Your Own Arguments

Your own feelings about the issue lend further strength to the argument. You may have new ideas that no one else has presented previously. Christopher Columbus could have written a persuasive research paper for King Ferdinand and Queen Isabella to convince them that the earth was round. His conviction that he could sail around the world, backed up with his experience as a sailor and navigator, could have convinced them to finance his voyage. You won't be expected to come up with anything quite so grandiose, but presenting something new and different is a vital aspect of your paper. You may have heard many references to "thinking outside the box." This is exactly what you do when you write a persuasive research paper.

Present Your Case Persuasively

You need strong, well-developed arguments in order for your paper to be effective. State what you think, and then back it up with reasons why you think that way. Use examples that show the reader a real-world application of your position. Suppose your paper were about the effects of living near high-voltage power lines. Your position is that living in close proximity to these power lines causes many serious health problems. You could find some news stories or interview some residents in these areas to show concrete examples of the health problems people do experience when they live near high-voltage lines. Explain what evidence you have that leads you to believe you are right. It is not enough to explain how you feel or what you think. A reader, and your instructor, cannot be convinced of your position unless you demonstrate why you think the way you do.

ALERT!

In a persuasive research paper, you do not present both sides of a debate extensively; you present just the side you are defending. To do this, though, you have to outline the opposing side so the readers get a clear picture of what the other option is.

Stage an Imaginary Debate

In a real-life debate, someone would provide a rebuttal to your case no matter how well thought out it was. Your opponent would never simply hear you out and then say, "Okay, you're right!" As you write your paper, try to imagine what a reasonable rebuttal would be. Which points could be attacked? Where are the weaknesses in your arguments? Think of objections that could be raised, and be ready to provide answers to them. Reinforce your points with more evidence or further ideas. You must leave readers with no doubt that you have provided a thorough argument for your case, even if the readers totally disagree with you.

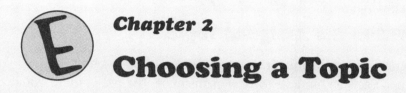

Chapter 2

Choosing a Topic

The first step in writing a research paper is deciding what it will be all about. This is a vital step. Your paper will be a central thought in your mind for the next few weeks or months or however long you have to complete the assignment, so you want to make a wise choice. The steps outlined in this chapter will help you to choose a topic that both suits you and satisfies your instructor's requirements.

Assigned Topics

In some cases your instructor assigns your topic to you. Rarely are these rigid topics. The very nature of research papers calls for some personalization, so usually you have some options within the topics provided. Occasionally the instructor provides a list of specific topics, and you choose from that list.

Choices Within the Assigned Topic

Sometimes an instructor assigns a general topic, but it is up to you to make a choice within that topic. For instance, the assignment could be to write a research paper about a composer from any time in history, which is a fairly broad topic. Suppose, for example, you chose Franz Liszt. Because this is a research paper, you still have many options within your topic. This is not a report, so you won't just present a timeline of the events in his life or write about the various pieces of music he composed, though you will include some of that information so that readers who are not familiar with his life or his music can follow your paper. Perhaps in your research you learn that he was the first pianist who seemed to have a sort of celebrity status. You learn that women screamed and rushed the stage when he played. A good research paper topic would compare the fans of Franz Liszt back in the 1800s to those of today's rock stars. From the initial general assignment of a research paper about a composer, you have chosen your own unique topic.

Make sure you know just how much choice you have within the assigned topic. Some instructors will let you do your paper on anything that is even remotely related to the assigned topic, while other instructors have much stricter guidelines. If in doubt, run your choice past your instructor for approval before you get too far into the project.

Be Unique

Although one of the reasons why instructors allow for some choices within a topic is because they want to avoid correcting a classful of research papers on the exact same topic, it is also to give you the opportunity to show your personality in your paper. Your choice of topics is a direct reflection of you, so try to narrow the topic to one that is unique to you. This is not just for your instructor's sake. If you do your research paper on the same topic as do other students, your paper will be compared to theirs. A paper that is the only one on its particular topic will stand alone, and therefore will be marked on its own.

Brainstorming for Topics

If you have the opportunity to choose your own topic with no restrictions, the options can seem overwhelming. Fortunately, brainstorming can help you through your dilemma. If you use the steps outlined in the following sections, you will have a topic in no time.

Write Down All Your Ideas

The first step is to get comfortable. Sit down either with a full-sized piece of paper and a pen, or at the computer. Clear your mind and workspace of all distractions. Then, write down every conceivable topic that comes to you. The important thing now is to write down every one. Don't do any editing right now. Write down the excellent ideas, the ridiculous ideas, the ones that seem too broad, and the ones that seem too difficult. Often, what you write down will bring to mind further related ideas. If you really allow the ideas to flow, you should be able to fill a page within a few short minutes. Take a break at this point. That way, you can look at your ideas with a clear focus when you begin the next step.

ALERT!

At first it can be hard to write down every idea without discarding the ones that don't seem good enough. Sometimes those initial ideas bring to mind better ones once they are written down. Remember that you have an entire page to fill, so every single idea gets recorded. With practice, brainstorming gets easier.

Narrow the Field

Now you can begin the task of eliminating the ideas you don't think would make for a good research paper. Look at each idea seriously. Ask yourself if each one is a topic you think is interesting. Do you want to know more about it? Would information be too hard to find? Is the scope of the topic far too difficult for you? Is the topic too limiting?

If some of the topics you wrote down are very broad, like soccer or animals, do some further brainstorming. Go through the process again, but this time just write down sub-ideas of that topic. For example, if you are doing further brainstorming on animals, you might consider a paper about endangered mammals, guide dogs, animal emotions, or unusual pet tricks. Then you can eliminate the ideas that you don't want to look into any further.

These ideas will be the basis for your research paper topic, but they are not likely to be the topic itself. Usually, at this stage your topic still needs some narrowing down and may take a slightly different direction. Before you reach that stage, however, you need to come up with a basic idea of what your paper will be about.

QUESTION?

What if I can't narrow it down to one topic or I don't really like any of these ideas?

If you can't narrow it down, don't agonize about it. You'll write more research papers in the future, so you might have the chance to use some of the topic ideas then. For now, pick the one that interests you the most or that has the most available information. If all else fails, pick one randomly. If you decide that you just don't like any of the ideas, continue on through this chapter for more suggestions. You can always brainstorm again; the topic doesn't have to perfect at this point.

Explore a Few Promising Topics

It is unlikely that you will immediately go from a full page of ideas to your final choice. You should, however, be able to narrow it down to two or three possibilities, or up to five at the most. From there you can do a bit more exploration to see which idea suits you best. Take the time to look up each one, either online or in an encyclopedia. Visit your library to see what you can find out about each topic. You are not doing serious research at this stage, but you are taking a quick look at how readily you can obtain information on these topics. You should soon get a feel for how much or how little is available. Something may catch your eye to convince you that an idea is not worth pursuing further, or that one idea is definitely the one to choose. Generally, after this exercise, you can narrow your choice down to one topic.

Choosing Carefully Without Wasting Your Time

It is understandable that you want to choose the best topic you can. Of course, you want to be able to find what you are looking for with a reasonable amount of digging, you want to learn something from the experience, and you want a topic that is within your capabilities. You also want to receive a good grade on the paper.

Begin Immediately

It can seem that the due date for your paper is a long way off, but don't put off choosing a topic. Let's suppose you are in a class that is assigned research papers on a Thursday, with the opportunity to choose your own topic. Another student does some brainstorming that same day, visits the library over the weekend, and by Monday morning begins work on his project. You, on the other hand, are so overwhelmed with the large project that you let it sit over the weekend. You do think about the paper, mulling it over and planning how to complete it. You also think about your choice of topic, but you don't take any concrete action toward choosing one. When Monday comes, you hear the other students discussing their papers and comparing notes. Once you realize that other students have already begun their work, you panic. Already you are falling behind. You quickly settle on a topic from your list. While the other students are able to complete their work easily in the remaining weeks, you anxiously center your life around the project in order to finish it on time, and you have a nagging feeling the entire time that your topic isn't the one you should have picked.

There is a moral to this story: Begin to choose your topic right away. Start the same day you are given the assignment if at all possible. There is no advantage to letting it sit for a few days; the topic is not likely to just pop into your head.

Choose Within the First Few Days

As you saw in the previous example, the length of time it takes you to choose your topic greatly affects when you can begin writing your paper. Therefore, it only makes sense to choose quickly.

The best way to ensure that you don't spend your entire project time trying to choose a topic is to set a deadline for yourself. If you follow the process set out here, you should be able to choose a topic shortly after the paper is assigned.

One caution: Though it's important to decide on a topic within a few days, it would be foolhardy to rush through this process immediately. This paper is going to be a major part of your life for the next several weeks, and you need a topic you won't be tired of in the first week. Choose quickly, but choose wisely.

ALERT!

If you are given a very short time frame in which to complete the entire paper, you need to choose your topic quickly—ideally in the first day, or perhaps in two days. Generally, the total time frame given for a research paper allows for a few days to choose a topic.

Writing About What You Know

This is often the first piece of advice given to anyone choosing a topic for any type of project. The advantage to writing about what you already know is obvious: You are researching a topic with which you already have a level of familiarity. You probably know where to look for information and may already know some experts in the field. In addition, you probably know what the key discussion points are before you actually do any research.

Hobbies

Think about the hobbies you pursue. Almost everyone has one or two favorite hobbies or activities they pursue in their spare time. Do you spend time knitting or woodworking or painting? Do you enjoy reading fantasy novels or playing games online? Do you grow your own herbs or play the clarinet or collect everything related to unicorns? Any one of your hobbies and interests is a potential starting point for a research paper topic.

Sports and Other Activities

We tend to think of sports involvement as only including organized sports, such as teams we play on or lessons we take, but this certainly is not where sports involvement ends. Though you may have a definite idea for a topic if you play basketball or excel at karate, thousands of other recreational sporting pursuits also could spin off into a research paper. Do you enjoy golfing? Have you ever played tennis? How about that time you went bungee jumping? Or got together with your friends to play paintball? These are also great starting points to choose a topic.

Other Areas of Interest

Sports and hobbies are not the only things you already know about. Maybe you have a part-time job that gives you some unique knowledge. If, for example, you work in a local electronics store, you may know all about computers. You may know which laptops are hot right now, or how to build your own machine.

You also may have family members or roommates whose jobs or interests inspire you. A brother who restores old cars or a friend who had a summer job fighting forest fires may have passed on some unique knowledge about these things to you.

Similarly, an event in your life may have prompted some interest or at least some knowledge. Suppose you broke your leg in the eighth grade. You might want to write about the long-term effects of a fracture, or about whether kids' bones heal faster than adults' bones do.

Writing About What You Want to Know

Sometimes picking a topic is not so much a matter of what you already know, but what you want to know. Your research then will be based on something that piques your curiosity. It is easiest to stay on track when you have a personal interest or stake in the topic.

People of Interest

Think of someone you admire. This could be a music star, a sports hero, a political activist, or your next-door neighbor. It could also be a historical figure, either one who is famous or one who is little known but still intriguing in some way. Perhaps you have a relative, alive or deceased, on whom your paper could be based. You could write a paper that describes the social or environmental influences that affected a specific aspect of that person's life or accomplishments. Writing about a person who is still living provides the special opportunity to interview that person, but you can still interview friends and relatives of people no longer alive.

Things You Would Like to Learn

Research papers provide you with a structured way to learn more about something that already interests you. These are the things that may have prompted you to say, "I wish I knew . . . " What better way to get to know all about that interest than by spending your research time learning about it? Having interest in your topic means you know it won't be dull.

Tying Your Topic into a Current Event

News events are a prime source of topics. Tune in to any television news report or read any newspaper or magazine and you will find a wealth of ideas. Whether you prefer international politics or the affairs of your local community, you are sure to mine stimulating and controversial issues in the media.

Today we have the distinct advantage over previous generations of knowing what is happening around the world at the moment it happens. Whereas hundreds of years ago people had to wait for a ship's return or a messenger on horseback for news from afar, we now turn on the evening news to see real-time images from across the globe. We log on to the Internet and read breaking news, or even read reports from sources in other countries. Although all this information can feel overwhelming, it does offer something of interest to each of us. Whatever catches your eye in the news could become the basis for a topic.

Your local news is inspirational in much the same way. No matter how big or how small your community, something will always be happening. Local issues are not limited to those affecting your city or town. Think both bigger and smaller. This also includes issues affecting your campus and your street, or your state or province. Because these local issues often have a direct impact on you, they can be much easier to get excited about. Also, you are close to the sources of information, which makes research a simpler task.

Choosing a Topic of Historical Significance

A topic that has to do with your community's history lends itself well to a research paper. Many times there are museums or historical sites where you can conduct research. The town or city hall is another good resource. Newspapers contain a wealth of information, and you can easily search them. You can quickly locate pictures from local sources, or you may be able to photograph or draw something yourself. Local residents can add more insight to your topic. You can discuss why your topic is significant and how the people or events in question affected the present or will affect the future. In short, local historical topics can be ideal.

Your Town's History

Begin by finding a brief history of your town. If you don't know much about it, ask if your local tourism office or chamber of commerce has this information. Museums and historical places of interest also can provide a more in-depth history. As you learn this history, think about the events and how they shaped your town. Major events, both naturally occurring (such as a tornado or drought) and human-made (like the railroad being built through town, or a big company pulling out of the area) can have a long-lasting effect. A lot of these events will trigger ideas for topics.

Early Citizens

Certain people from your town's past also are a good source of topic ideas. Commonly, these are the well-known people for whom various landmarks around town are named; they are the residents who contributed something of value to their community or were influential in some way. Don't limit yourself to the better-known citizens, however. If you can dig up information on a more intriguing person from the past, it can make for a very interesting research paper.

Don't forget to make use of the memories of some of the long-term residents of your community. Friends, neighbors, and relatives might be able to vividly recall important events from years ago. This could save you from spending hours trying to uncover an interesting historical event. You'll be doing something nice for someone, too—elderly residents often welcome an opportunity to share their memories.

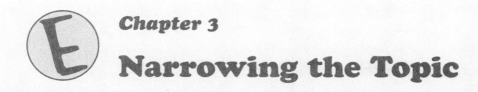

Chapter 3

Narrowing the Topic

The topic you have chosen at this point is still a fairly general one. Now the task is to fine-tune that choice and narrow it down until it becomes a specific and original topic. This leaves you with a project that is both interesting and manageable.

Ensuring That Your Project Is Unique

The narrowed topic that you choose will be something that is unique to you. You will make the choice based on your own particular interests, knowledge, and opinions. The topic will become yours and yours alone, because no one else would put the same personal slant on it. Your goal is to modify and refine a general idea into a topic that is exclusively yours and truly reflects your personality.

Compare Notes

You may be in a class of thirty students or a lecture hall of more than a hundred students. Whichever the case, it is to your benefit to ensure that your project topic is not the same as that of others in your class. Obviously, in a large class it may be difficult, if not impossible, to find out what every other student has chosen for a topic. Nonetheless, your objective should be to talk to as many other students as you can to ensure that your topic is different from others.

There are many reasons for this. First, if an instructor receives several papers on identical topics, it would be almost impossible not to compare them to one another. A project that is the only one on a particular topic is judged on its own merits. It can be compared to a quality standard, but this is not as definitive as comparing it to another project on the identical topic.

Of course, you may not know that others are researching the same topic as you are at the same time. This is particularly true if your topic is based on a current event or a hot controversy. This is all the more reason to begin your research immediately. If you procrastinate, the good sources may already be taken.

Second, it makes sense logistically to do your project on a unique topic. Some resources, such as encyclopedias and almanacs, may be available to more than one person. Other resources are limited in number. Suppose your project deals with a local historical figure who was the subject of a few documentary films. As luck might have it, your local library has a copy of each of those films available to take home for a period of six weeks. A class-mate discovers this first and signs out all the copies, leaving nothing for the rest of you. Similar incidents could happen with books, letters, videos, and other research material.

The same goes for an interview subject. A person integral to the topic you are researching may be quite happy to grant an interview to one student. However, if five students request an interview, this person won't be as likely to oblige. Keep your topic unique to you so that the sources are available just to you.

Use Your Personal Beliefs

One of the best ways to make sure your topic is uniquely yours is to use your own background to help you narrow the topic. Do you have a strong opinion for or against a certain issue? If, for example, you feel that hunting is a humane way to manage wildlife overpopulation, your feelings may go against those of many of your peers. They may feel that hunting interferes with an ecosystem's natural chain of events. Your beliefs could form the basis of a research paper that would be yours alone, especially if in fact your opinions were different from mainstream opinion.

Your personal feelings are important in this type of project. Therefore, any topic that enables you to fully express those feelings is ideal. This is also the case when your feelings are similar to popular opinion, as long as you can add your unique thoughts on the topic, and in your own words.

Do you have special knowledge about a topic that may uniquely qualify you to offer an opinion about it? Perhaps you made your initial choice of topic based on something with which you are familiar. This strategy can also work for narrowing the topic. You may have chosen to do your research paper about playing the violin because you have played since you were four years old. This is using your knowledge to pick a general topic. Then you may decide to narrow the topic to a comparison of the different methods of teaching violin because you tried three different methods before finding the one that worked best for you. This demonstrates using your knowledge of a specific aspect of that general topic to decide on a final topic.

ALERT!

Even if your topic is one you are very familiar with, you still need to do extensive research. There will be facets of your topic with which you are less familiar. You can always learn more about any subject. Don't assume that you know it all.

Do you have an interest in learning more about a particular area? Again, you may have used this consideration when you picked your broad topic. It certainly makes for an interesting research experience when you are learning more about a topic you wanted to learn more about anyway. If you have always wanted to know more about Native American cultures, that may be the basis for your general topic. You might not be interested in all aspects of every tribe, though. Your interests may lie in the ceremonial dancing, or in what life is like on a reservation. Your unique interests will result in a topic that is interesting to both you and the reader.

Funnel Your Ideas

As was the case when you were brainstorming for a general topic, it can be helpful to write down all of your ideas as you narrow the focus of your topic. Think of the process as funneling. You begin with a broad idea, and slowly funnel it down to one narrowed portion of that idea. To visualize this, write your general topic idea across the top of a page. Below that, write the related subtopics that interest you. You are doing a form of brainstorming in this exercise, so again you should write down everything that comes to you. Don't worry about discarding ideas that you might not want to pursue. Under each subtopic, again write down any ideas for a more narrowed topic. Continue with this process until the topics you have are as narrow as is feasible for a research paper. At this point you need to choose one of the narrowed topics to be your research paper topic.

Asking Questions to Narrow the Focus

One of the easier ways to narrow the focus of your research paper topic is to brainstorm by asking questions. Many research paper topics seek the answer to a question. Often a question will bring to mind a related question, so the narrowed topic you choose may end up being a combination of questions. Asking questions about various aspects of a topic is a sure way to come up with a variety of ideas for narrowed topics.

Who?

Most topic ideas can have a "who" question related to them. You could ask who will benefit from something or who will suffer because of it. You could ask who discovered something. You could also ask who was the first or the last person to do or use something.

Let's look at an example. You have chosen climbing Mt. Everest as your general topic. In order to narrow this topic you could ask questions such as "Who are the Sherpas who aid in these climbs?" or "Who were the people who attempted to climb Mt. Everest but failed?" You could ask who the youngest climbers were, or the oldest climbers. You could ask who died attempting to make the climb. The "who" questions always center around the people involved with that topic.

QUESTION?

Does each idea I include have to be a narrower subtopic of the one above it?
This is the general idea, but not a strict rule. You are trying to narrow the topic as you go along, but if a related idea comes to mind, write it down.

Why?

The "why" questions are often both the most difficult and the most interesting questions to brainstorm. We all want to know what motivates people to do the things they do. Sometimes, though, it is difficult to imagine things being other than they are, because we are so used to filtering things through the same lens. You could ask why something happened or failed to happen. You could also ask why a certain issue is important or why it has the support of the public. To get yourself thinking of "why" questions, consider how something could be different, and then ask why it is not.

Where?

Obviously, "where" questions are related to location. This type of question can ask where something occurred or where it is most prevalent, where an idea came from, or where something should happen next. If your general topic is space travel, you could ask "Where should private commercial space flights travel to?" or "Where in the world are conditions most favorable for space landings?" You could ask "Where are private spaceships built?" or "Where did private spaceship designers receive their training or get their ideas?"

When?

Your topic may involve a time frame. You could ask questions about when an event is likely to occur next if a specific time isn't known, such as the next time a volcano is likely to erupt. You could also ask questions of this type about the past, particularly if no specific answer is known. You would deduce through your research when the event in question most likely occurred, but there would be no definite answer that you could look up.

A "when" question doesn't always make for a good topic. It is important to ask open-ended questions when you are asking this type of question. Too easily, you could come up with a research paper topic that would be answered without much room for interpretation or discussion. Avoid asking a question that has a limited answer.

How?

"How" questions may be the ones most appropriate for a research paper. With these questions you can narrow the topic by probing how things work, or by finding out how long, how often, or how many as the questions may pertain to your topic. A look at some potential research project topics shows that "how" questions can highlight many aspects of a general topic. If your topic were mountain goats, you could ask how mountain goats walk on cliff faces without falling, how often they do fall, how mountain goats have used their natural habitat to aid in their survival, or how the mountain goat family compares to the human family.

Narrowing Your Focus as You Gather Research

It is ideal to have your narrowed topic chosen before you start to do research. What is ideal, however, is not always feasible. There are times when it is necessary to begin to gather research before you have completely narrowed down your research topic. At these times you will narrow the focus of your topic as you progress through your research.

When the Focus Isn't Apparent

You may not have narrowed your topic before starting your research simply because you are having difficulty figuring out what the focus should be. There are times when ways to narrow the topic are very obvious. One choice may stand out above the others as being the one closely suited to you, the one with the most information available, or the one that will hold both your interest and the interest of the reader longer. Sometimes several perfect options present themselves, and your only challenge is selecting one. At times like these, the task of narrowing your topic is much easier.

Unfortunately, at other times the opposite is true. You may know that you want to write a research paper on a certain general topic, but the focus of that topic may not be readily apparent. You may have difficulty identifying your options for narrowing the topic. Sometimes you just can't come up with the one definitive branch of your general topic that you want to explore further in your research. In this case, it would not be in your best interest to spend any more time narrowing the topic. Begin your research on the general topic, but keep in mind that eventually you will need to narrow it. Often the focus you should take becomes more apparent as your research progresses.

If you're having difficulty finding a focus for your paper, it could be helpful to spend some time browsing through a *Web portal* in your topic area. Portals show various topics broken down into subtopics, each of which is linked to Web sites containing additional information on that subject. Doing this could give you ideas for narrowing your topic that you never thought of. Many search engines are also Web portals, the most familiar being Yahoo! If you find yourself on a Web site that includes many links to further information on a wide range of topics, or includes other services such as e-mail, shopping, and forums, you are likely at a Web portal.

Refocusing

For one of several reasons, you may find that you need to change the focus of your topic. For instance, you may learn that you had misjudged the amount of information available to you, or you may realize that the topic is much smaller or larger than you had anticipated. In any case, it would be most prudent to refocus your topic within the same general topic. Much of the background research could be similar, so you would not have to start at the beginning of your research again.

ALERT!

Make sure that you only refocus your research project topic when absolutely necessary. It can be very tempting to simply switch topics whenever you run into difficulty. In order to progress through your project, you need to stick with a topic whenever possible. If you truly identify a need to refocus, narrow the topic as quickly as you can.

Is the Information Available?

There is one vital step left to take before you settle on a research project topic: you must be sure that the information you need is available. This is not to say that it won't take some digging to find that information; often the research that you do will be far more involved than any you have done before. But if you are researching a topic that simply does not have information available, you will end up frustrated.

Unrecorded History

If your topic involves tracking down historical information, you usually will have a number of different avenues for research available to you. However, sometimes the specific information you are looking for just isn't recorded anywhere. You can check through letters, documents, photos, or other records and still come up empty-handed, because some things are never chronicled. Events in question may have occurred prior to the lives or memories of anyone you can interview. If this happens, refocus on a related topic that is recorded in some form.

Secret or Classified Information

If your topic deals with crime or the military, or even some areas of the government, you may not be able to gain access to the information you want. Such information is only available to certain people. You will need to decide if this type of information is necessary to your research, or if you can still continue with your topic without having this information. Depending on your topic, you may be able to find enough unclassified information to continue, or you may be able to draw your own conclusions and then carry on by using them. Some records must be released to you under the Freedom of Information Act. Requests for disclosure of these records must be in writing, and the Act is subject to several exemptions, so not every type of document or record will be available to you. Keep in mind that the Freedom of Information Act does not apply to every branch of government; it applies to the executive branch of the U.S. federal government, but not to local governments or to Congress.

FACT

Government information is commonly labeled as belonging in one of five categories: top secret, secret, confidential, sensitive but unclassified (referred to as protected in some countries), or unclassified. Information in the first three categories is sometimes called classified information. Some countries only use four categories, dispensing with the sensitive but unclassified label. Only information and documents in the unclassified category are released to the general public.

Don't Get in over Your Head

Your research paper will be due on a specific date. That means your topic needs to be one that you can research and write about in the amount of time you have available. Some topics may be great choices, but if they cannot be done to the best of your ability in the available time, there is no point in pursuing them.

Though it may not initially be obvious, too much information is a problem. If you find yourself overwhelmed by your research, you probably took on a topic that is just too large in scope. If you have so much information that you have no idea where to begin and know that you will never use more than a small portion of it, you have a topic that is too big. You should narrow the topic some more so that it will be manageable within the time frame you have.

It is also common to find yourself with a topic that is too difficult for you. You may indeed be interested in your topic, but it might be beyond your capabilities. For example, you might wonder how Fermat's last theorem was solved by a mathematician a few years ago, but unless you have a very strong math background, you can't adequately cover such a topic. Difficult topics often involve reading highly technical information, and they may require knowledge of special terminology. Unless you already possess the necessary knowledge, it would be too time-consuming to delve into a topic of this magnitude. Though you may have to shift your topic to something more suited to your level, you don't need to completely discard that topic area. Choose a related topic that is within your capabilities, but still challenging.

Projects Too Narrow in Focus

The opposite problem can also occur. You may have put so much effort into narrowing your topic that you went too far. Some projects are too narrowly focused and cannot be completed as is. These project topics have to be expanded upon to allow you to research and write a a full research paper. For example, if you were researching the effects of chocolate milk on hyperactive children, the focus would be too narrow, but the effect of sugar would have merit as a topic.

Not Enough Information

If you come to a dead end when gathering your research, your topic is too narrow. Maybe you can get bits and pieces of information, but you need a lot to fulfill the requirements of your research paper. Take the time to explore all the materials that you feel should contain the information you seek. Then, if you still think that your topic is lacking in available information, you need to broaden your topic.

If you used the funneling technique when you narrowed your topic, it should be a simple step to back up a level. The topic that led to the narrowed one you chose is quite possibly appropriate. Probably this broader topic has enough information available. If you picked your topic without the use of the funneling technique, you can probably still broaden yours a little to find a topic that will work. Occasionally you may need to choose an entirely different topic.

QUESTION?

How will I know that I don't have enough information?
It should be apparent if you still have questions that are unanswered or if you look for data or details that you are unable to find. It isn't so much that the volume of information is low; the problem is that it won't cover all aspects of your topic.

Gather Related Information

If you find that your topic is too narrow in focus, the best solution may be to gather the related information that you do find. Your actual topic will require some fine-tuning after this, but will end up being related in some way. For example, suppose you decide your research paper topic will be "Are Floor-Cleaning Products Harmful to Pets?" After some careful research, you realize that not enough data is available. You begin to gather any related information you come across. As you progress you find there is sufficient information on cleaning products in general, and that most studies have been slanted toward babies and toddlers instead of pets. Your eventual topic becomes "Are Chemicals in Common Cleaning Products Harmful to Young Children?"

Take a Step Back

Sometimes, when we are too involved in something, it is hard to see that thing clearly. This can happen with research projects as well. You may believe that you are trying to research a topic for which there is not enough information, but it's possible to miss an obvious research source because you are concentrating so closely on one aspect of the project. At other times there really is not enough information. Then it can be difficult to pick out an obviously related topic or broader topic. Take a step back from your project and try to look at it from the viewpoint of an uninvolved person. Better yet, ask a friend or someone else who is not involved with your project for an opinion on what you are missing. Sometimes it is just a matter of getting a fresh outlook at what is right in front of you.

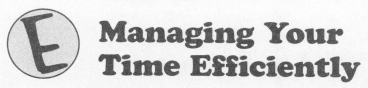

Chapter 4

Managing Your Time Efficiently

A research paper is a big test of your time-management skills. Not only are there multiple tasks involved—everything from library research to interviews to rough copies and editing—but you also go through this process independently. The time from the beginning of the assignment to the due date is basically yours to manage. It must be used wisely, because you rarely have much, if any, cushion.

Reasons for a Schedule

As soon as you receive the assignment for your research paper, you need to draw up a schedule. Few people are able to work effectively toward a deadline without setting a schedule for themselves. Many manage to complete the task on time, but only after spending a few long nights catching up on what they know they should have worked on earlier.

Create Manageable Tasks

A schedule divides your project into manageable tasks, each with a realistic deadline. Instead of working toward a completely finished project by a certain date, you will work toward a series of goals within that project. For example, it is much easier to reach a goal of finishing the editing on your rough draft by next Tuesday and then adding some maps and drawings by Friday than it is to vaguely know you have to do that plus much more in the next ten weeks.

Avoid Procrastinating

People procrastinate for a variety of reasons, but the reality is that there is no time for procrastination when writing a research paper. Some people are so intimidated by such a large project that they can't seem to get started. They can be so afraid of failure that they are unable to get themselves motivated. Other people are confident they can do a good job, but they want the paper to be perfect. These are the ones who get hung up on picking the best topic or on gathering more research than they possibly could use. They can never get on with writing the research paper because they can't get past each step until they feel it is flawless. Still others intend to do the paper but allow too many other things to get in the way of their work.

Despite what some people think, procrastination is simply a bad habit. It is not a learning disorder or a personality disorder, and it is definitely not laziness. Furthermore, people who procrastinate can learn how to stop, so that it does not become a lifelong habit.

Schedules work well for anyone, regardless of work style. Those who are afraid of failure find it easier to deal with one step at a time, instead of tackling the whole project. Perfectionists benefit by the reminder to move on in order to keep up with the schedule. And those who have problems making time for their research paper are less likely to let things slide until the last minute because they can see how the project needs to progress at specified times.

If you are a procrastinator, you can sometimes force yourself to work on something you keep putting off as a way to avoid something that you are even less inclined to do. Suppose you are writing a research paper about the health benefits of chocolate milk. You keep putting off the research until you get an assignment in calculus that is much more work. When you sit down to get some work done, you are now more likely to do the research about chocolate milk, because you don't want to do the calculus assignment.

Creating Your Schedule

You now know why you need to schedule and what could happen if you fail to do so. Next you need to gather information so that you can create your schedule.

ALERT!

It is imperative that you know the exact due date. Don't rely on what you think you heard, and don't rely on the word of others. Be sure you have it in writing or get it directly from your instructor. This is vital. You can't afford to plan your project based on the wrong date.

Know the Due Date

The paper's due date is one of the most important pieces of information given to you, but it's also one that's easy to miss. Without this date, you will have no way of knowing whether you are on track to finish on time.

Your first task is to double-check the due date. You may have written it among your notes if the instructor gave the assignment orally. If not, look at the printed information you were given. This information may contain details about the project's requirements, including the minimum length, what the project must contain, and how it should be formatted or presented. You should be able to find the due date among this information. The course syllabus that you received at the beginning of the term may list major assignments, including your research paper, and the due dates for them. If you have checked all these places and are still unable to find the due date, ask your instructor.

Write It Down

Make it a point to record the due date on the Research Paper Schedule in Appendix A. You also should record the date on a calendar or in an agenda book or PDA as a continual reminder of how much time you have remaining to work on your project. A calendar that's printed on a wipe-off board can be ideal for scheduling, because you can easily make any changes as you go along. The format you use for your schedule is a matter of personal preference. What's most important is that you must write down your schedule in order to stay accountable to it. A schedule in your head is not concrete enough to keep you committed.

QUESTION?

What if my instructor tells me she wants to see something that I have scheduled for later?
Each instructor does things slightly differently. If yours wants to see something by a certain date, then make sure you have it ready in some form by that date. You can always make revisions later.

Mini Due Dates

Some instructors assign mini due dates. They may want to see your rough draft by a certain date. Some may ask to see your research notes. Others will only give you the final due date and not look at any of your work other than the finished product. No matter how much you may want to work through the assignment on your own, these mini due dates are to your advantage. They help you to motivate yourself, which is especially valuable if this is an area you have trouble with. They also ensure that you are on the right track with your project, both in terms of the type of information you are including and the time frame in which you are completing everything. Some instructors will give you helpful suggestions after they see the work you have done, particularly regarding sources for further information and extra details you might want to include. Make sure you know each of these mini due dates. They are just as important as the final due date.

Where to Begin

You now have a specific start date, a specific end date, and possibly some mini due dates. The next step is to determine whether it is easier for you to work your way forward or backward through the schedule. You may discover that you have a preference, or you may find it makes no difference. Unless you would rather do it differently, start with the date you can begin work on the project and work your way through, keeping an eye on the due date. It will usually take a few tries before you come up with a schedule that allows enough time for each task. You can adjust the schedule to allow for either more or less time once you have it tentatively written down.

What to Schedule

Look at the topic you have decided on, and figure out what steps you need to take to complete the project. Use the chapters in this book as a guideline for what is required. Then mark the final due date on the Research Paper Schedule in this book or on a calendar. Add any mini due dates your instructor has given you. Starting from today's date, write in every step that you will have to complete. Give yourself sufficient time to complete each step, and spread out the tasks through the days you have available. Keep this schedule in a convenient place so that you can refer to it frequently to ensure that you are on track.

Other Homework and Commitments

When making up this schedule for your paper, you need to take into account other parts of your life. First is the fact that your research paper is not the only homework you have. You probably are taking other classes that require regular homework. You may have large projects to complete during the same time period for another class, and you may have exams to study for. You need to allow time for this other work. Even if you don't have a clear idea of how much other homework you will have, you can probably make an educated guess about how much time it takes every night, on average, to finish your work. You can also ask your other instructors if they plan to assign something that might coincide with your research paper.

You are likely to have other commitments that you should build into your schedule. Do you have a job? Are you on a sports team, or do you participate in a recreational activity on a regular basis? Have you already made plans with family and friends that you should honor? Be sure to consider all commitments that you already know about when you make your schedule. After considering these other commitments, you might realize that there will be days when you have no time at all to work on your research paper. There is no point in thinking that you will make progress that day if it is just not possible.

Setting Goals

Goals are closely tied in with the schedule you make for yourself. You can have a schedule without goals, and you can set goals without a schedule, but they are so intertwined that you may as well do both. Goals can help you in many ways as you work your way through your research paper. In fact, without goals to work toward, you would find it very hard to complete your paper on time. Setting goals allows you focus your efforts on each goal in succession and helps you manage your time.

Setting goals is basically the same as setting up mini due dates for your project. You divide up the work that you need to get done in order to complete the research paper and decide when you will complete each section. These mini due dates are just a series of goals that you plan to meet.

There are many personal benefits to having goals. Learning to set and reach goals helps you gain skills that will benefit you in your future career and in your everyday life.

Goals and Motivation

When you are first faced with writing a research paper, the entire project seems immense. The best way to deal with this is to divide the paper into smaller tasks, or goals. That way you aren't looking at finishing the entire paper all at once. Instead you are working to accomplish each smaller goal, one at a time. A smaller goal is less intimidating, and therefore you will find it easier to get motivated to work toward it than you would be to work toward a larger goal. The series of goals is basically a plan for completing your paper. With this plan in place you can focus your attention on each task rather than on what all of the tasks are and when you need to finish them. You'll be surprised how effectively these smaller goals move you toward your ultimate goal.

Characteristics of a Good Goal

You should avoid setting goals haphazardly. There is no sense trying to work toward a goal that you don't have any chance of achieving. Good goals need to have a few characteristics in order to be useful. They need to be attainable, specific, and measurable. Make sure that every goal you set has all of these characteristics to ensure that the goal is helpful to you.

Is It Attainable?

A goal should be challenging, but it also must be one that you can reach. If you know that you have no chance of interviewing a high-profile celebrity, for example, don't set the interview as one of your goals. The idea of setting goals is that you will accomplish each one in succession and then move on to the next one. If you fail to reach your goals, you will find it difficult to know when to set them aside and continue on.

Is It Specific?

You need to be specific when setting goals. Decide what exactly it is that you want to achieve. For instance, don't just decide that you want to get halfway through working on your research paper. What is halfway? Do you mean halfway in terms of the time the entire project will take, or halfway in terms of the research you must do? A more specific goal states when you want to complete the library portion of your research or when you want to finish proofreading your first draft.

Is It Measurable?

The goals also need to be measurable. That is, some time frame must be associated with them. It is not enough to set a goal of finishing a certain part of your project without setting the exact date that you are going to finish it. You will generally set goals that deal with completing specific aspects of your paper. The fact that they are to be complete is also a measurable part of your goal. For example, a good goal might state that you will complete writing the first draft of your research paper in twenty days. This goal is attainable, specific, and measurable.

How Much Time to Allot per Task

It is always difficult to estimate how long it will take to complete a task. Students often grossly underestimate the amount of time it will take them to do a job thoroughly. In order to come up with a reasonable schedule, you must be fairly accurate with the amount of time you allow per task. Obviously, you can adjust the amount of time suggested for each task here if you have less or more time than what is usually allotted for a research paper.

The time that is recommended for each task is only a suggestion. You may work faster or slower on certain tasks than you do on others. Your particular project may not include some of the tasks, or others not included here may be required. Adapt these suggestions to suit your particular case.

Choosing the Topic

Choosing and refining your topic should be a minor part of your research paper in terms of the amount of time it takes. Ideally you would finalize your topic within a few hours of receiving the assignment, although most people need more time than that. You do need to limit the amount of time you spend on this task, so set aside only two or three days to choose your topic, narrow the focus, and perhaps shift the focus slightly if required.

Doing the Research

You might be surprised to learn that research is usually by far the most time-consuming part of your project. You probably will spend at least half of the time you have left for your project gathering research. To make this task seem less daunting, take some time to figure out where you are likely go for your sources of information. You can then schedule a few days for encyclopedia research work, a day or two to visit museums, another couple of days for interviews, and so on.

Don't underestimate the amount of time you will need for research. This is the basis of your entire paper. It is important that you gather enough information to completely cover your topic. If you try to cut corners, it will show, and the result will reflect poorly on you.

Creating the Outline

Once you complete your research, you need to organize it and put it into the format you want for your research paper. It is difficult to estimate how much time you will need for this part of the process; however, it is best to err on the generous side. Some research papers are quite easy to organize based on the topic and type of information you find. Others are more difficult, and some may even require going back for further research or clarification. Try to determine as best as you can where your paper falls between these two extremes. Then you can allow yourself anywhere from a few days to a week to complete your outline.

Writing the First Draft

It seems that writing the first draft would be time-consuming, but if you have taken careful notes (in your own words—see Chapter 12!), and outlined your paper in detail, it shouldn't take all that long. This step is really just a matter of putting all that work into sentences, adding your own interpretations and opinions, and ensuring that it all hangs together. A week should be plenty of time to write the first draft.

Proofreading Your Paper

This is an area that students sometimes skim over. Careful proofreading and editing is not something that can be done in an hour. Take your time with this task and do it properly. You will want to give yourself enough time to put it away for a day or two and then reread it, because a fresh pair of eyes can almost always catch mistakes. You may also want to get someone else to help you proofread, so schedule at least three days for this task.

Completing the Final Draft

The final draft shouldn't take a lot of time. Using the rough draft as a guide, you just make corrections and add or delete to improve your paper. Most sections will not have to be rewritten and reworded. But do leave yourself enough time to do a neat job on your final draft. A couple of days will result in a higher quality finished product than will a couple of hours.

Allowing for Distractions

Your research paper is a big assignment, and it will be a big part of your life until it is completed. But it certainly will not be the only thing in your life, which means that you need to allow for other things when you schedule your time. Allow time not only for your other homework and commitments, but also for distractions that will come up from time to time.

QUESTION?

What should I do if there isn't enough time to complete everything before the due date?
You'll have to work that much quicker. See if there are any tasks that you can cut back on by a day or two. If that still doesn't make a difference, show your schedule to the instructor. He or she may have a suggestion for getting back on track. Avoid asking for an extension. It is unlikely that you will get one, and even asking reflects poorly on you, no matter how great your paper is.

Your life includes friends and social outings, which can be distractions that are hard for some people to manage. Continue to have a social life, but keep in mind that you have made a commitment to stick to your schedule whenever possible. If you find that your social life is causing you to slip behind on your project, it is time to prioritize things better.

A sport that you participate in on a regular schedule is quite simple to allow for in your schedule, but other spontaneous activities, such as impromptu basketball games or long online gaming sessions, are more likely to cause havoc. Moderation is always the key. You don't want a research paper or any other assignment to take over your life. Other interests are important too. Just remember to balance your other activities with the task you need to complete in time for your due date.

Life being what it is, things will come up unexpectedly to throw your schedule off. These can include a personal tragedy or something else that requires your immediate attention. There may even be a national or international event or crisis that demands your attention and concentration. Things can and do go wrong, such as accidentally deleting the rough draft you typed into your computer, and this is another good reason not to cram your work into the last bit of time before the due date. You need to allow for the possibility of things going wrong so that you have time to deal with it if it does happen to you.

It is helpful to build some leeway into your schedule. Always assume that it will take you the longest possible amount of time to complete a task. If you think you might be able to finish the outline in three to five days, allow five days for it if time permits.

You may also find it helpful to not schedule right to the due date. Work under the assumption that something will always happen to slow you down. Schedule your time so that you complete writing the paper a few days prior to the due date. Then if something goes wrong or if a task takes much longer than planned to complete, you will have a few days to spare.

Revisit the Schedule

At specific points throughout your project, you should take a look at how you are progressing against your schedule. Check the various milestones along the way as you complete major groups of tasks. For example, look at it after the research is done, after you have the outline ready, and after you write the first draft. Check your progress to make sure you are still proceeding as you should be.

ALERT!

If you have fallen behind, you may need to make some adjustments. At any of these points you might also realize that some of the upcoming tasks will take either more or less time than you had planned for. Adjust your schedule then so you can see how the change affects the overall timing.

What to Do If You Get Behind

Despite your best efforts, you may find yourself slipping behind. Perhaps you misjudged the amount of time to allow for a certain part of your project. It may have been a very tight schedule to begin with. Maybe something happened in your life that completely ruined your concentration for a period of time. Or maybe you just did too many other things when you should have been working on your project. So what do you do now?

ALERT!

You can't reschedule over and over again. That would defeat the whole purpose of a schedule. Reschedule when unexpected circumstances cause you to fall behind, but don't use rescheduling as a solution whenever you don't want to make your schedule a priority.

If it is still early enough in the process, you may be able to set a new schedule. Take the remaining tasks you have, and the remaining amount of time before the due date, and fit the work in evenly. You will have to work all that much harder and more efficiently from that point on because there won't be as much, if any, leeway in your schedule. You won't be able to allow as much extra time for other activities or for unexpected events.

If you are really struggling with finishing the amount of work you have in the amount of available time, you should ask for help. Some instructors are more approachable on this than others. Again, you want to avoid asking for an extension. What you might get is some guidance as to whether you are headed in the right direction or are spending too much time on any one area, and which aspects, if any, you could leave out. If asking the instructor for help isn't possible, sometimes tutors or peer mentors can offer assistance. An added advantage is that they are typically older students who have recently tackled similar projects.

Chapter 5

Encyclopedias and Other Reference Materials

The first stop on your research journey is the encyclopedia and other types of reference volumes. You probably are quite familiar with these resources from working on previous reports. Students often neglect other reference tools available to them because they either don't realize that the sources exist or they don't know how to use them properly. In addition, you may overlook some materials because you mistakenly assume that they would not be suitable for your research.

Encyclopedias

Back in the early grades of elementary school, when you were first introduced to report writing, your teacher probably led you to a set of encyclopedias in the school library. You learned how to find the correct volume for your topic, and how to find your topic within that volume. These are basic research skills that you are now ready to build upon.

FACT

Print encyclopedias range greatly in size. Some are only one volume, while others take up entire shelves. The *Encyclopaedia Britannica* is the largest general encyclopedia in the English language—thirty-two volumes containing more than 44 million words and more than 24,000 photos, illustrations, and other visual aids.

Locating Encyclopedias

You may be lucky enough to have a full set of encyclopedias in your home. These large encyclopedias usually come in sets of twenty or thirty books arranged alphabetically. They are a major, but worthwhile investment. Even an old set is still useful, because much of the information does not change. Just be careful to augment what you find with updated statistics on populations, country boundaries, and so on. Any school or public library has at least one set of encyclopedias on hand, and often has many different sets. These are usually just for use in the library, so you need to set aside the time to take notes from them while you are there.

More recent encyclopedias are also available on CD-ROM or DVD. These generally contain the same information, but may also include video clips, sound clips, and Web site links. As with all computer technology, new advances continually add to the diversity of these encyclopedias. Though even now they contain a greater variety of types of information, and are much cheaper to purchase than are the print versions, they do have some disadvantages. The most obvious are that you have to have a computer to use one, which means that you also need a power source, and only one person can use the encyclopedia at a time.

Most of the major encyclopedias also have online versions. These usually are much smaller versions of the encyclopedia, but they still include the most popular topics. Many of these online versions charge a subscription fee for access, and have the same disadvantages as the CD-ROM or DVD. On the other hand, they are generally updated as new information becomes available, whereas CD-ROMs and DVDs are updated only when they are next published.

Special Encyclopedias

Encyclopaedia Britannica and the *World Book Encyclopedia* may be among the better-known encyclopedias, but they certainly aren't the only ones. There are many, many more, and some are more specialized. You should be able to find these special encyclopedias in the reference section of a library. Each one deals with a specific subject. These range from the *Encyclopedia of Philosophy* to the *Automotive Encyclopedia* to the *Encyclopedia of the Orient*. In a project about natural disasters, you might use the *A Narrative Encyclopedia of Worldwide Disasters from Ancient Times to the Present*. This would provide in-depth information specific to the chosen topic to add to the general information found in the more common encyclopedias.

What to Look Up

The obvious thing to look up in an encyclopedia is a keyword or keywords describing your topic. For a research paper about clouds, you would not only look up "clouds"; you would also look up "weather," "meteorology," and so on. But keywords are not all you can find in an encyclopedia. The index, which may be in the last book of the set or in a separate volume, contains all other references to those terms. When you look up "clouds" in the index you may also find that there is information about clinometers and cloud seeding in the encyclopedias. It would be a mistake to end your encyclopedia research after simply looking up the entry for the main topic.

You also can look up names of people associated with your topic. (Remember to search by last name, of course.) In addition, you can find relevant information under listings for countries or cities or any other related, but relevant topic.

Some encyclopedias, especially those written with students in mind, contain leading questions at the end of every topic. These are very applicable for research papers because they prompt ideas for further exploration. They also might lead you to further focus your paper.

QUESTION?

Where will I find all these reference materials?
You have several options. School and university libraries are usually well stocked with reference materials, because that is what their students require. Public libraries, especially those in big cities, also have an abundance of reference works. Bookstores stock the most recent publications, but you generally have to order encyclopedias directly from the publisher or from a salesperson.

Almanacs

Almanacs are often overlooked but are a highly useful reference tool. Unlike encyclopedias, almanacs were probably never mentioned to you for report writing. This is a great loss, because almanacs contain a large amount of information and statistics. For most projects you can find an almanac that contains information to contribute to your work.

ALERT!

Almanacs often contain some very interesting bits of information. While you probably never thought it would be fun to read an almanac, it is easy to get sidetracked as you scan the book. Try to stay focused on your research and save the pleasure reading for another time.

What Are Almanacs?

Almanacs are usually single volumes published once a year. They contain facts and information about such a wide variety of topics that they are somewhat hard to define. One of the more popular almanacs is *The World Factbook*, but again, you can find specialized almanacs for extremely specific types of information. You probably have heard of the *Farmers' Almanac*, which is used primarily for weather forecasts and planting information.

Types of Information

If you need recent statistical information, an almanac is the source to use. A general almanac has statistics on everything you can imagine. The top news stories of the year, military pay scales, life expectancy in all countries, drugs prescribed most often, high-school graduation rates, and a list of Nobel Prize winners represent only a tiny sampling of what you can find in an almanac. Some information is from the year in question; other information is historical data.

QUESTION?

How can I find what I am looking for in an almanac?
Information in almanacs tends to be organized under very general headings, so it can be difficult to find what you're looking for. Almanacs typically contain a general index with subheadings. Think of large headings that your topic might be found under, and then look them up to see if your topic is one of the subheadings.

For a project about home computers, you may find information in an almanac on the percentage of households with home computers, the dollar sales per year of computers, and the top-selling software programs. You may not know at this point if you will eventually use all the information, but it may be helpful to jot it down to aid in further research.

Dictionaries of All Types

A dictionary may seem a strange tool for research. After all, don't you just look up words in the dictionary to find their meaning or to make sure you are spelling them properly? Actually, you can find quite a lot more information in a dictionary than that.

Standard Dictionaries

A pocket dictionary can be fairly limited in the amount of information it includes, but a regular desk dictionary, one of those thick volumes you find in libraries, includes much more. Commonly you will find the origin of a word. This includes the place of origin as well as the original meaning. Some dictionaries also include a brief encyclopedic entry. Though this may repeat the main information you find elsewhere, occasionally you will learn something new. Depending on the word, alternative words or names could be listed so that you will know what else to look up. The front of a dictionary contains a section describing how to use it. This section includes examples showing all the information listed under each word and how to interpret the listing.

It is imperative that you look up the proper spelling and the proper form of a word in the dictionary. Often students say a word isn't in there because they are trying to spell it incorrectly. Other times they could be looking up the wrong form, so that, for example, they are finding the noun instead of the adjective.

Specialized Dictionaries

As with encyclopedias, you can find dictionaries for many specialized areas. Words that are peculiar to a certain topic may not be included in a regular dictionary because the words are too specialized. Make sure that you don't miss the dictionaries associated with your topic area. There are law dictionaries, foreign language dictionaries, sign language dictionaries, medical dictionaries, investment dictionaries, and music dictionaries. As with most reference materials, there also are several specialized dictionaries online.

Atlases

An atlas is a collection of maps put into a book, but as with other reference books, you can find much more than you expect in most atlases. You probably have an atlas of some kind at home, or at least in one of your classrooms, but check out the library for its selection. Atlases are not all the same.

Standard Atlases

A typical atlas will include both political and physical maps. Political maps show country borders and major cities. Each country is shown in a different color, making it easy to distinguish among them. Some pages display maps of a single country with each state or province shown in a different color. Physical maps show land types—for example, tundra, rain forest, and desert. They also show elevations in a visual form, with each level of elevation or depth a different color or shade. An atlas may also include environmental maps that show farmland, urban centers, forests, and barren land.

The information doesn't stop there. Some atlases have encyclopedic information about the solar system and the stars. Some include maps of the continental shift, showing how the world possibly looked millions of years ago and how it could look millions of years in the future. They may show explanations of geographical and geological terms such as those pertaining to rivers and waves, ocean currents, landforms, and types of rocks. Some contain maps of the ocean floors, showing all the trenches, basins, and seamounts. And usually there is a section listing statistics about each country, with the capital city, area, and population.

ALERT!

A globe also can be useful at this point in your research. Though it doesn't provide the variety or quantity of information that an atlas does, some people can better understand the visual representation of a globe. Some globes are three-dimensional, with ridges to indicate mountain ranges, and dips for the lower elevations.

You may wonder how you can use the maps you find in an atlas. You can use them to see where an event took place or where a famous person was born. You can calculate what the distance is from one place to another. Country boundaries sometimes change quickly and frequently, and rural areas become urban ones, so a look at historical maps can help. If your topic involves ancient times, you will find that the mapmakers' impressions of how the world looked is almost unrecognizable compared to the accurate maps drawn today. Finally, you can add a map as a visual aid in your paper to illustrate how a place or type of land influenced or had an impact on the subject of your paper.

Specialized Atlases

Specialized atlases focus on one particular area. There are historical atlases that show only maps from different times in the past. Population atlases show patterns of population growth by year and by location. Animal atlases show the different species of the world and where they live. A biblical atlas shows where all the events in the Bible were said to take place. In short, you may be able to find an atlas specifically devoted to your topic. Suppose you are writing a research paper about astronomy. A search of the public library might yield not one, but five atlases of the stars. While much of the information may simply reiterate what you already found in encyclopedias, one of the atlases may contain something completely novel. In short, don't rule out any sources because you assume they won't provide you with valuable information. You won't know for sure until you check them out.

Other Reference Books

You're still not finished with the reference section. This is why entire floors of main libraries are devoted to reference material and are staffed by reference librarians. A good library contains a vast amount of reference material that goes far beyond encyclopedias and other basic references.

There are many reference materials not mentioned here that could be useful to you. These include telephone books, business indexes, gazetteers, maps, books of quotations, flag databases, census data, and more. A reference librarian can help you find all the sources available in your particular library.

Directories

A directory is a basically a listing of resources. There are directories for innumerable topics, and new directories are published every year. Many times you will find that a directory leads you to another source for further information. There you will find the contact information for that source and can take the next steps to learning more from it. When you contact each source, explain that you are a student doing a research paper, and briefly describe the topic of your paper. Most organizations are happy to provide you with what you are looking for, and sometimes will even assist you with more than you originally ask for. For instance, if you were researching the reaction of victims after a natural disaster, you could find a directory of world relief organizations. You could then write or phone each of them asking for specific information about past disasters and stories of how people reacted. From these contacts you might get a much more personal perspective on the events than you could from the factual information that you read. In addition to sending you information or answering your questions directly, some of the contact people may allow you to interview them, and you could receive photos or other printed material.

Yearbooks

A yearbook is similar to an almanac in that it is printed each year. However, a yearbook contains information specific to that year only, and usually is confined to a narrow subject. A well-known example of a yearbook is the *Guinness Book of World Records*. Libraries generally have the past few years of any yearbooks they keep in their collection, and they can usually locate a yearbook for a specific year you are looking for.

You may find that your topic spans many years, and that you need to look at a specific type of yearbook for each of those years. Make sure that the information you believe you will find in the yearbook is worth the time it will take you to search through all those volumes. Could you find the same information in an almanac? Will you just be duplicating the facts you already researched? Suppose your topic deals with the progressions made in space exploration over the years and whether or not their expense is warranted. You could look up information in a yearbook such as the *Guinness Book of World Records*. There you would find facts about the longest manned space flight or the largest planetary rover, which could be relevant to your paper. These facts obviously would be updated as the years go by, so you could check this book from different years to see how and when the information changed. However, this information could also be available from a single source that would also include other details, such as costs. In this specific case, you might try to obtain information directly from NASA, or you could look through a space almanac.

Reference material is available in an almost overwhelming amount. This is true of all reference sources, not just yearbooks. Make sure that you find all that you need, but don't go overboard and waste valuable time on this segment of your research.

FACT

Yearbooks are not always for a calendar year. Just like school yearbooks, they may follow a different range of dates. This could be a seasonal year or a fiscal year or whatever range suits the topic.

Thesauri

Though a thesaurus doesn't seem like a logical tool for research work, it can help in subtle ways. You can sometimes get stuck looking up the same word or words every time you search for information. Because you are so close to the situation, it is often hard to see which related terms you could be searching for. This is where the thesaurus comes in. If applicable, look up the words you are using to determine whether any of the related terms that the thesaurus provides could be useful to you. For example, for a research paper about headstones, you might find gravestone, cairn, and interment. This gives you other terms to use in your research.

Calendars

A calendar can be an indispensable tool for certain topics. Many calendars include much more than the basic form you hang on the wall to keep track of days and dates. There are historical calendars for any year in history. Some calendars contain information about special religious days, public holidays from any country around the world, and notable births, deaths, and events on each day in history. You can find ancient calendars, zodiac calendars, and calendars that have information about phases of the moon, sunrise and sunset times, and changes of season.

ALERT!

Keep in mind that these reference materials provide only the background facts to your research. These sources are an essential part of your research paper, but they do not offer any evaluation or interpretation of the information they contain. That will all come from the further research you will do as well as from your own thoughts once you have collected the background information.

Chapter 6

Books as Research Tools

All the emphasis on exploring different sources of information may lead you to forget about a prime source of research: books. There are millions of books, and they cover every subject imaginable. There must be one, and probably are many, about the subject you are researching. What you need to know is how to find the books that will be useful to you, and how to get the information you are looking for from those books.

Using Libraries to Find Books

The obvious place to begin looking for books is the library. You can use the public library, the school or college library, or even the private library of a large company (with permission, of course). Don't limit yourself to the one library you have always visited. You probably can find many other libraries too, and most are open to students if you ask. Now you need to know how to use the library to find the books you require.

Of course, once a book is published, the information it contains won't be updated unless a revised edition is published later. Be sure that the information you are taking from a book is not outdated. You can revise your information by checking with a more up-to-date publication, such as a magazine or newspaper.

Card Catalogs and Computer Searches

When you look through the library for books about a particular topic, you use a keyword or subject search. You aren't likely to know the book's title or its author unless it has been recommended to you. The topic you are searching for may fall under more than one keyword or subject. If you are researching toxic plants, you could look up "plants," "gardening," and "toxicology." Then you could also look up specific varieties of toxic plants, such as "poinsettia, "philodendron," and "tulip bulbs." Once you do some of the research work, you may learn of related subjects that you can search for.

Most libraries began the change from card catalogs to computerized catalogs sometime during the 1980s. Most have phased out their card catalogs completely, although a few retain them as a record of their older books and of their rare book collection.

Libraries generally use one of two different types of catalogs. The older type is the card catalog. Most libraries have done away with this system now, although you may still come across one occasionally. Because you are far more likely to use a computerized catalog, the old-fashioned card catalog is not covered here. If you do happen to encounter one, don't worry—they are "self-service" and very easy to use. If you have any problems, ask a librarian to help you.

You are more apt to find a computerized catalog system at your library. This system is really just a card catalog on a computer. You look for a subject index, and then search for the keywords you think are applicable.

Call Numbers

The number that is shown for each book in both the card catalog and the computerized catalog is the *call number,* which usually is derived from the Dewey Decimal System. Call numbers are a way of classifying books into categories. This allows similar books to be grouped together in the same part of the library. That makes it easy for you to browse for other books on the same, or a similar, subject. The Dewey Decimal System organizes books as follows:

- 000 to 099—General Subjects
- 100 to 199—Philosophy and Psychology
- 200 to 299—Religion
- 300 to 399—Social Sciences
- 400 to 499—Language
- 500 to 599—Pure Science and Mathematics
- 600 to 699—Technology or Applied Science
- 700 to 799—The Arts
- 800 to 899—Literature
- 900 to 999—Geography and History

If your topic is "The Differences Between Catholicism and Protestantism," you can look directly at the shelves that contain call numbers between 200 and 299 to find books pertaining to religion. Within each section of the Dewey Decimal System, the classifications are further broken down. For example, languages are found between 400 and 499, but each number in that range is designated for a specific subject within languages. For example, etymology is 412, German grammar is 435, and Classical Greek usage is 488. You can see how this system places similar books side by side on a library shelf. In a library, the call numbers are posted at the end of every row, on every shelf, and on the spine of each book.

QUESTION?

Does every library use the Dewey Decimal Classification System?
No, but it is the one used most often. Another popular system is the Library of Congress Classification System. It is a newer system that also classifies books by subject area. Libraries with large collections of research work are likely to use the Library of Congress system.

Using the Librarian's Services

Librarians know where everything is in the library, and they are there to help you find what you need. Librarians can help you with specific requests if you already know what you are looking for. They can also suggest other resources available in the library that you may have missed. In addition, they can often obtain materials for you from other libraries, sometimes from other states. This can be a huge benefit if you live in a smaller city or town that has a modest library.

Ask for Help

Remember that librarians are not commissioned salespeople. They will not ask if you need assistance. They will not ask you later if you have found what you are looking for. You need to ask them if you want help. Otherwise they will assume that you know what you are looking for and how to find it, and that you want to be left alone. Librarians have made it their career to research. Therefore they know how best to find what you need quickly. They know what sorts of information are available, and whether you are looking for something that simply doesn't exist.

When you ask librarians for assistance, you need to be clear about what you are searching for. Tell them in detail what type of information you are hoping to find. Let them know what the topic of your paper is. Tell them what information you already have and what you think you are missing. Ask if they have a particular resource. Librarians are much more likely to be able to help if they know the specifics of what you want. They would also like to know that you have done as much work as you can on your own. They won't be as willing to go out of their way for you if they think you are looking for an easy way to get someone else to do your background work for you.

FACT

Many larger libraries also offer an online service whereby you can ask a "virtual" librarian for help, which can be very useful if you are unable to get to a library for any reason. University libraries and even the Library of Congress offer an "Ask the Librarian" service on their Web sites. You generally will receive an answer within a day or two, often sooner. Such services are frequently free, or available at minimal cost.

For example, suppose you are doing a research paper about laser eye surgery. If you tell a librarian that you want everything they have on that topic, he or she probably won't be of much assistance. The librarian is likely to either give you the call number of that subject or show you where to look it up yourself. Now imagine another scenario, in which you do some background work before you ask for help. You are able to tell the librarian that the topic of your paper is "What Are the Long-Term Risks Associated with Laser Eye Surgery?" You tell the librarian that you have already taken notes from encyclopedia articles and books about the process involved in laser eye surgery. You have interviewed a local eye surgeon and have requested pamphlets and brochures from nearby laser clinics. In addition, you have read a few related articles in medical journals. What you would like to find at this point are some recent studies of long-term effects that people have suffered as a result of this surgery. A librarian will be more than willing to help you under these circumstances because you have been specific about your needs and you have proven that you have already done much of the work yourself.

Check Back Later

Librarians can't drop everything they are doing whenever someone requests some help from them. Sometimes they are able to help you immediately, but at other times they may note your request and get back to you later. Depending on the library policy and on the type of search they are doing for you, either they will contact you or it will be up to you to check back later. Make sure you do this.

Nothing is more frustrating to the librarian than to put a lot of effort into helping someone with research only to find that the person can't be bothered to return to get the results. If you happen to find the information elsewhere and decide you no longer need help, let the librarian know.

Finding What You Want in a Book

You've found the books in the library that pertain to your topic. Now it is time to sit down to take notes from them. How do you find the information specific to your research topic in these books? Obviously, not everything in the books is directly related to your exact topic. But there is no way you have the time to read each and every book from cover to cover. You need to employ some skills to locate the information you are looking for in a timely fashion.

Table of Contents

The most evident place to look is each book's table of contents. If you are lucky, your precise topic may be the subject of an entire chapter. Some chapter titles are plainly worded, in which case you will know right away whether a chapter is relevant to your topic. Sometimes, though, you have to decipher chapter titles because they use jargon or slang peculiar to the topic, or they obscure the chapters' contents in some other way. In any case, read through the table of contents and check out any chapters that you think might contain information you can use.

Index

The index, which is at the back of most nonfiction books, is much more detailed than is the table of contents. Here you can look up your subject in the same way that you searched through the library's catalog. Under each entry in the index you will find one or more page numbers for discussions about that particular subject. An entry may have subcategories if information about them appears in various places throughout the book. For example, a book about organizing has "planners" as one of its subjects in the index. Subcategories of the "planners" entry include "choosing a planner" (found on pages 139–41), "size" (page 139), and "write it down in" (pages 150, 151). When the page numbers are separated with a dash, as is the case with "choosing a planner" on pages 139–41, that means this is a continuous section that begins on page 139 and carries through until page 141. When they are listed with a comma, as in the subcategory "write it down in a planner" on pages 150, 151, that means there is a mention on page 150 and another mention on page 151. This section does not carry straight through from one page to the next.

You also may find that looking up one subject in the index leads you to another, related subject. Suppose you were to look up "center forward" in a book about soccer. The index gives you the page numbers where you can find references to "center forward," but it also tells you to "*see also* striker." Now you know that if you look up "striker," you will find further related information.

ALERT!

Book indexes are arranged alphabetically, which should make a topic easy to find. However, there is always the chance that you will be using a word to describe your topic that is not the word used in the index. Try to think of other terms that could be used to describe your topic, and look up all of them.

Looking at Related Books

If you only look at the books on your subject that you find in your local library, you are missing out on a vast amount of printed information. It's likely that many other books contain something about your topic. They may take some searching to find, however.

Sources

Many people don't realize that not every library houses the same books. If you have enough time, you should visit every library in your vicinity. Some libraries are connected to other nearby libraries as part of a system, which usually allows you to conduct searches for books that are located at any library in the system. If you find a listing for a book that is at another library, that library can send the book to your library for you. Sometimes libraries will arrange for interlibrary loans, whereby a book can be brought in for you from another, unrelated library.

QUESTION?

Can I sign books out of another library system?
The rules will be different from one library to the next regarding which books you can sign out. Check with each library in question. Make sure that you return books to the library from which they were borrowed.

Search Related Topics

When you look for a book about a particular topic, it can be hard to pick out what you should look for besides that obvious topic. If you are doing a research paper about the inventions of Thomas Edison, you may have found a few books about Edison in the library. There may be other books about inventors in general on the same shelf, and they may have useful information in them. You can find them without having to go back to do another search. Because similar books are shelved in the same area, you can just look at the other books nearby on the shelf. The same concept can help you when you are looking up a related subject. While doing the project about Edison, you probably also searched for books about light bulbs and phonographs. There may be related books on those shelves as well. It may not even be apparent at first that a related book has anything you could use in it. Look up your subject in the index of a related book to see if the book could be of use to you.

Other Sources for Books

You already know that libraries are a wonderful source of books both old and new, as well as other research material. Do you know that bookstores are great sources as well? Even the largest, most well-funded libraries can't keep up with the pace of publishing. Bookstores are terrific sources of information, even when you are just browsing.

Bookstores tend to stock mainly newer titles, but you often can find a selection of both new and older books, including titles that have not yet been purchased by the library. Larger cities often have bookstores that specialize in books of a certain genre, such as architecture or self-improvement. As in the library, if you don't find the exact book you are looking for on the shelf, other books nearby may be just what you need. Megabookstores with café seating are perfect for quiet browsing. If you can't afford to buy a book that you think would be helpful, consider asking your local library to purchase it. Few people realize that their community library is often happy to do that, although you may have to wait a few weeks for it.

ALERT!

If you are looking for books that are no longer in print, one of your best options is to search on the Internet. Using a resource such as Bibliofind ✍(*www.bibliofind.com*) or Alibris ✍(*www.alibris.com*), you can search for out-of-print, rare, and used books that may be difficult to find in a bookstore or library.

Don't overlook used books as resources. You can find used books not only at used-book stores, but also at garage sales, flea markets, and on eBay. Whatever the location, finding books that pertain to your topic takes a lot more digging. There are no systems for searching through these collections other than to just look through them all. The reward can be a great find, however—an obsolete or out-of-print book that contains an interesting and different view of your topic.

Chapter 7

Magazines and Newspapers

If your research involves looking for time-ly news information, you should use all the magazine and newspaper sources you can find. Libraries store magazines and newspapers for many years. There are thousands upon thousands of magazines and newspapers. Luckily, this isn't just a hit-and-miss type of research. You can search the content of these publications quite eas-ily if you know how.

Choosing the Right Magazines

You quite possibly buy magazines regularly. You might even subscribe to one or two. Depending on the degree to which your interests mesh with your research paper topic, you may already have on hand some magazine articles that could aid you in your research. Be aware that magazine articles generally don't cover issues in as much depth as do other types of sources. They often are written at a novice level, so they touch on a lot of general information without going into the details. They also tend to be slanted toward the writer's opinion. This is not always a bad thing for your purposes. You want to uncover different points of view that either support or oppose your own. Just be sure that you know what is fact and what is opinion. Despite these cautions, magazines are still great sources of tidbits that don't surface elsewhere.

Consumer Magazines

Consumer magazines are the ones you probably read most. These are the ones sold at the grocery checkout counter, at the drugstore, and at the newsstand. They appeal to a wide audience of readers and deal with a surprising variety of subject matter. Some of these are general in nature; others are highly specialized. There are enough consumer magazines to fill entire stores, and it seems that every subject has at least a handful of magazines devoted to it.

Make sure you can differentiate among consumer magazines, trade magazines, and professional journals. The audiences are different, and therefore the material covered can take a different slant. Consumer magazines allow for a lot more interpretation and personal input from the writer, although facts are never modified.

With this profusion of magazines, it's likely that there is at least one related to your research topic, and probably more than one. An advantage that magazines have over books is that they often are published monthly, or at least quarterly, and sometimes even weekly. Each issue has many different articles, product reviews, letters, photos, and short fillers. They can run from thin publications barely larger than a newsletter to thick volumes containing more than a small book. That all adds up to a large number of potential articles related to your research topic.

Trade Magazines

Trade magazines are less well known, but that does not mean that there are fewer of them. Trade magazines are those published specifically for people in a particular trade or business. Do not confuse these with professional journals. Trade magazines are written in the same easy-to-read style as is a consumer magazine. The information in a trade magazine covers new developments in its field, more efficient ways of working, and profiles of interesting people or companies within the trade. There are magazines for trades as diverse as interior decorating, avionics, teaching, chemical engineering, and pharmaceuticals. With such a wide range of subjects, there should be a trade magazine applicable to your research paper topic.

Depending on your topic, you may be able to find the magazine you want at your local library. Larger magazine retailers carry many of the more popular trade magazines. If you know that a trade magazine is available for a certain subject but you can't find it anywhere, contact the related trade organization.

Magazine Indexes

Once you've identified the magazines you want to look at further, you still have work to do. You can't possibly search through every issue from every year the magazine was published to find the odd article that may pertain to your topic. It would be like looking for the proverbial needle in a haystack. Luckily there are such things as magazine indexes.

Each magazine usually publishes its own index in some format. You can look through the indexes for the issues you think are most likely to contain articles of use to you. Another option is to look through the comprehensive magazine indexes that reference many different magazines. The reference section of your library should have copies of these—in particular, the *Reader's Guide to Periodical Literature*. You can use this guide to search for your topic and then for which issues or volumes of which magazines include articles with something related to that topic.

To make it even easier, most public libraries and even some school libraries have access to magazine indexes on computer. There are many different types of indexes, and they have many different names, so you should ask the librarian for help to find out what they have and how to use them. You can find some of the indexes on CD-ROM or DVD; others are online. You can sometimes even access them by going to your library's Web site.

ALERT!

If your research uncovers a magazine or newspaper article from a time in the past when the article was breaking news, make sure you also retrieve all follow-up articles. There could be retractions of statements that were made, or further developments that change the information in the original article.

You can search the electronic indexes in much the same way that you perform an Internet search. You type in the keywords closely associated with your topic; the results you receive are those that most closely match your keywords. The results give you information much like what you see in a bibliography: the name of the article, the name of the magazine in which it appeared, the volume of the magazine, and the page numbers. Some systems also show you the name of the writer, and the month and year of the magazine, which is often easier to find than is the volume number. In some cases your search will retrieve the full article. If not, you at least know which issue of which magazine you need, and what page to look at once you get it.

Be aware that some search results will be for articles contained in magazines or journals to which you must subscribe in order to view or download the article. If that's the case, get the article from the library instead.

Searching Current Newspapers

Newspapers, particularly daily newspapers, can be the best source for up-to-date news. They cover a wide range of topics and report nearly anything that's newsworthy. Make sure you double-check the accuracy of newspaper stories by cross-referencing them with those in another newspaper or elsewhere. If you do that, however, be sure to check the source of the second newspaper's information. We live in an era of media monopolies; don't be surprised if the second source got its information from the first source!

Local Newspapers

If your topic is related to a local issue or has some sort of local connection, your obvious choice would be a local newspaper. Luckily, this is an easy search to do. If you are concerned with news that is still breaking while you write the paper, you can simply do the research as the news happens. If you are looking for newspapers from a short time ago, visit the newspaper office. It is likely to have the most recent back issues. Reporters may have extra information that wasn't necessary for their stories that they can pass on to you, or they may be able to put you in touch with other sources. Another handy feature of a local newspaper office is that it will sometimes sell you glossy prints of photos taken for stories it ran. These are usually not the same ones that were published, and the price is generally fairly low.

Some major newspapers also sell black-and-white historical photos from newspaper stories they ran far in the past. These are more expensive than the fairly recent ones, but they make a great addition to a research paper if applicable.

Events are not the only things published in a newspaper. Advertising can lend an insight into the daily life of a particular period in time. The quantity of Help Wanted ads can tell you whether unemployment was high or jobs were plentiful. Companies often publish information about the promotions of employees to key positions. Obituaries can tell you details about a person's life that were never made public before. Letters to the Editor can tell you what public opinion is on a particular issue. Public opinion can also be expressed in editorial cartoons, but make sure you give full credit to the cartoonist if you use a previously published cartoon in your paper.

National and International Newspapers

If your topic is beyond the local scope, you should look through national or even international newspapers. Sometimes these can still be purchased locally, but it is certainly not as easy to get ahold of back issues or to visit the newspaper office. Almost all newspapers of every size now have their own Web sites, making it easier to read the news from around the globe. However, back issues are usually only available for a limited time, and even then the cost can be prohibitive.

Your best bet is to go to the local library once again, and search through older newspapers there. Bigger libraries often have a room devoted just to newspapers. In one section of this room you'll find a shelf of newspapers from around the world. The most recent one is often displayed, but sometimes there are a few older issues behind or underneath that one. Keep in mind that you can only use these newspapers in the library, and usually just in the newspaper room. They cannot be marked up or cut up, but you can take notes from them. If you're in a hurry or the library is about to close, consider copying the information you need.

FACT

Newspapers in the United States were originally published on a cotton rag fiber paper, leading to the expression of calling a newspaper a "rag." These newspapers would have lasted almost forever, but because the papers were very expensive to produce, the publishers switched to the cheaper but less durable newsprint.

Searching Old Newspapers

Once you go back further in time than a few weeks or months, you'll have to use other techniques to search old newspapers for information. This is true whether you are looking at local, national, or international newspapers. Obviously there is no library in the world large enough to store all the newspapers ever published, and even if there were, newspapers are not durable items. Luckily, there are techniques to preserve these newspapers in some form.

Microfiche

If you aren't already familiar with microfiche, visit the newspaper room at the library. There you will see large machines with big screens that look sort of like an adaptation of an overhead projector. These are the microfiche readers. All those old newspapers are transferred onto a small film so they can be stored. You can only view these films by using a microfiche reader. This reader magnifies the film on a lit background so it can be read. Once the image is enlarged onto the screen, you can scroll up and down or from page to page. The readers aren't complicated to use, although you will probably want to get the librarian to show you how to use it the first time.

Some libraries may have their old newspapers on microfilm. This is very similar idea to microfiche. Microfilm readers look more like a computer, but the basic concept of being able to read an old newspaper on a screen is very much the same.

ALERT!

Don't limit yourself to looking only for older copies of currently published newspapers. Like other enterprises, newspapers also go out of business, and many of the historical ones didn't survive to the present day. Your librarian may be able to help you find a newspaper that was published during the era or in the location that is relevant to your topic.

Search By Date

Newspaper searches are easiest when you know the exact date of the event in question. For a research paper about tornadoes, you might do some background research and learn of a very destructive one that occurred near Xenia, Ohio, on April 3, 1974. These are important details to aid in your newspaper search. You now know the exact date and the place. Newspaper stories beginning the following day from Xenia and the surrounding communities would all contain details about this tornado. They would also include details of the impact on the town and the citizens' reactions to the disaster—just the sort of stories you are looking for. If you don't know the exact date of an event, you may be facing a long search, so try to pinpoint it as accurately as possible.

Newspaper Indexes

As with magazines, newspaper stories also are indexed. Most libraries carry newspaper indexes from the major newspapers as well as the local newspapers. Because newspapers are printed so often, these indexes also are updated often. Newspaper indexes work in virtually the same way as do magazine indexes, and you can search newspapers using the same computer indexes that you used for your magazine article search.

Other Periodicals and Journals

Adding to this wealth of information are still more publications. The following sections briefly describe some additional types of publications that might be useful for your project. Of course, not all of these are relevant to every kind of topics, so you might use only a few of these sources.

ALERT!

Don't waste your time trying to decipher professional journals that are clearly over your head. You may be able to find a trade magazine for the same profession that contains the same information in more understandable terms. Or perhaps it would be easiest to interview a professional who has read and can explain the journal you want to use.

Professional Journals

If you feel capable of understanding technical information, search out a journal printed for professionals in your topic area. Professional journals include information about new techniques and research discoveries, so they can be an intriguing source. The technical level of the writing is often quite high because the journals are directed to people who are deeply involved in a profession. Therefore, even if you can understand these journals, keep in mind that your reader may not. Be sure to carefully paraphrase any technical information into language that the layperson can understand.

Travel Brochures

Though you may feel ready for a holiday after you are finished with your research paper, that is not the real reason for using travel brochures in your research. The brochures are valuable if you are writing about a particular country or region, and they may even include information about a specific attraction or the customs of another culture. Travel brochures are not likely to contain in-depth material, but they may touch on something you haven't considered before.

Government Brochures

All government agencies, from the national level down to the local level, regularly publish a number of brochures. Each government department usually distributes informational pamphlets that deal with the department's area of responsibility. The purpose of the booklets usually is to educate the public, but they also sometimes include statistical information or information about new regulations and guidelines. You can generally obtain the publications directly from government offices, and they are either free of charge or relatively inexpensive. Thousands of different brochures are published by government agencies, so chances are good that you can find at least one pertaining to your topic. For example, if your paper deals with how parents can help keep their children from experimenting with drugs, you could order *Growing Up Drug-Free* from the U.S. Department of Education. Your librarian can help get you started, or you can try Google from home. You could also check the Web site of the U.S. Government Printing Office at *www.gpo.gov.*

Service Organizations

Service organizations are those usually nonprofit volunteer-driven groups that work to support a specific cause or a number of causes. These include such groups as United Way, The Nature Conservancy, and Habitat for Humanity. The groups publish a surprising number of newsletters and brochures, some of which may be useful to you.

Newsletters

Newsletters for these organizations usually come out monthly or quarterly, depending on whatever schedule each organization has set out. They often are distributed only to organization members and to donors. If you think a particular newsletter could contain information helpful to your research, you can contact the organization directly and ask it to either add you to its distribution list or send you specific newsletters that contain the information you request.

QUESTION?

How would I know that a particular newsletter from a service organization has any information helpful to my research?
You probably wouldn't know unless you heard about it from someone else. Failing that, you could contact an organization relevant to your research and ask whether its newsletter contains information about your very specific topic.

Informational Pamphlets

Service organizations also print information pamphlets that may be easy to obtain. The purpose of these pamphlets is to inform the public about how the organization works for its cause and, sometimes, to solicit donations. You usually can find these information pamphlets in many public locations, at events sponsored by the service organization, and even in your mailbox. The mailing address of the organization is usually printed on the pamphlet, so if you think it may have further information applicable to your topic, you can always write to the organization. Some service organizations, especially those dealing with medical conditions, also put out free fact sheets. These often are available at your local health clinic or your doctor's office.

Other Publications

Some of the larger service organizations publish their own magazines. For example, Optimist International, an organization aimed at bringing out the best in kids, publishes *The Optimist* magazine. Magazines such as this often highlight activities of the various branches of the organization, and some of these activities could be relevant to your research.

Some service organizations also offer other unique publications. Myvesta, a nonprofit consumer education organization, puts out audio- and videotapes that mainly provide financial advice, such as paying off debt and using credit cards wisely. If your topic were related to money management, you might want to send away for these to find out whether they would be of use to you.

Public Newsletters

Groups other than service organizations also distribute newsletters that could be helpful in your research process. These newsletters, which are circulated to the general public, come from a wide range of groups and associations and cover just as wide a range of topics. Your biggest challenge may be finding out what is available.

Public newsletters are published by so many groups and offices that it can be difficult to pinpoint which ones might apply to your topic. You may already be aware of some of the more visible newsletters. They are often distributed free of charge at any place that is open to the public. For instance, a newsletter put out by the mayor of your city might be found in the lobbies of municipal buildings. Your local school board may put out a newsletter that it leaves at school offices and its own board office for any interested people to pick up. A reference librarian may be able to help you search for these types of newsletters. There are a variety of periodical directories, and many of these include public newsletters along with magazines, newspapers, and journals. Some of the smaller local newsletters won't be listed here, however. For these you will have to look in every public location you can think of. If you have an idea of who might possibly publish a newsletter relevant to your topic, ask that person or organization. Even if the person you ask doesn't publish a newsletter, he or she is closely involved in that subject area and probably knows what is available.

In addition to the large number of newsletters available in print form, you are likely to find an even larger number available by e-mail. Often known as *e-zines*, these are becoming increasingly popular as more people go online. However, because anyone can start an e-zine and there is little to no cost involved, the reliability of the information contained in these e-mail newsletters will vary greatly. Verify all the facts that you uncover from these sources. Usually you can read through all the back issues of the e-zine as well as sign up to receive it on a regular basis.

ALERT!

You can find a public e-mail newsletter or e-zine easily by searching for it in any search engine. For example, a search for "real estate investing newsletter" brings up more than 1 million pages. Of course, after reading this book, you will know how to refine all those results!

Private Newsletters

Private newsletters are those that are distributed just to the members of a group or association. For example, a university alumni association distributes its newsletter to all graduates of that university. Though it may seem that these would not be available to the public, they actually can be easy to find. They may be referred to as private newsletters, but that in no way means that the general public is excluded from reading them. Because such newsletters are generally produced on a tight budget by the sponsoring organization, and may even be published on a volunteer basis, there is no funding for a large distribution. Members of the organization are obviously the most interested parties, so they are the ones who get the newsletters. But in most cases the organization can provide an extra copy to any person who requests it, especially if it is for academic purposes.

Finding Out What Is Available

Private newsletters may be easy to find simply because the organizations that produce them are so narrowly defined. The newsletters themselves won't be listed anywhere. You have to contact the groups to ask if they do in fact produce a newsletter and what types of information are included in the newsletter. This last point is important. You only want to pursue a newsletter that will provide relevant information that you haven't uncovered elsewhere. You have no need for a newsletter that covers only trivial information, information that you already have, or information unrelated to your research topic.

How to Obtain Them

Once you have determined that a specific group publishes a newsletter that could help you, call or write to request what you want. If you have already made contact with someone from the group personally, request the information from that person. Otherwise, send a letter, which is less likely to be ignored. Let the group know whether you want copies of previous newsletters, or want to be put on its distribution list. Of course, if the newsletter is only published quarterly, you may not receive one before your paper is due!

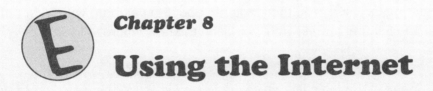

Chapter 8

Using the Internet

During its brief history, the Internet has revolutionized the way we do research. Mountains of information are available to us from our computers—at home, at school, even on the air. Much of this information simply wasn't available to the average person just a few short years ago. What was available took many hours of searching at libraries and elsewhere through thick volumes of reference material. The Internet is a marvelous tool, but unless it is used wisely, it can be frustrating and inaccurate.

Where to Look

It is easy to believe that the Internet is going to make your research life easy because all of that information is out there, just waiting for you to access it. However, you may soon find out that this is not the case. In fact, instead of waiting for you, sometimes it seems that it is hiding from you, slipping from your fingers just as you think you are about to catch up with it. In order to use the Internet for research, you need to know where to look.

Many of the materials already discussed in this book, including encyclopedias, reference materials, books, magazines, and newspapers, are also available on the Internet in some form. Be aware, however, that some of these sources are sometimes "lighter" versions of the printed material, so though they may still contain some basic information, they may not present the material in its entirety.

Search Engines

Search engines are the main tools to use to find information online. This is especially true if you are searching for a topic area you have not searched for before and you are not already familiar with the Web sites that provide this type of information. For example, suppose you decide to pursue a project on cod fishing. When you begin your project you feel compelled to find out more about the depletion of natural cod stocks and how that has affected the lives of cod fishermen. You have heard stories of long-term unemployment and depression due to the loss of this livelihood for many fishermen. You want to find out whether this is a common reaction or an anomaly picked up by news reports. Despite the fact that you have a strong interest in the topic, it is not one you have ever researched before. You have never seen a Web site that has any information about cod fishing, and have only once or twice happened upon a news site. It is in situations such as this that a search engine becomes your most valuable research tool.

A search engine is similar in some respects to a phone book or an encyclopedia. Search engines are basically directories (huge directories) that retrieve information you have specified from a database. You enter the search terms or keywords just as you would look up a name or subject in a phone book or encyclopedia. Phone books and encyclopedias, however, take you directly to the information you are seeking. A search engine provides you with a list (a very long list, usually) of Web addresses, including brief summaries, that might contain the information you want.

FACT

As with most things connected with the Internet, search engines come and go with dizzying speed and frequency. Google is the most commonly used search engine at the time of this writing, and we even talk about "Googling" a keyword instead of searching for it. Despite this rapid incursion into our lives and vocabulary, Google has only been in existence since 1998.

So many people today are using Google as their main search engine that they often forget that many others are available, and the options keep changing. Yahoo!, Ask Jeeves, and HotBot are also worth noting at this time. Most search engines work in much the same way, but it is still worth reading through each search engine's help page to see if it offers any unique features. Search engines usually also have a section called "Advanced Search Techniques," or something similar. These are worth looking at, because they usually offer advice that helps you refine your search or look for images.

Because of the ever-changing nature of the Internet, search engines sometimes become portals, and portals sometimes become search engines. The two are closely intertwined, so it can pay off to go back to visit one or the other if you haven't been there in a few years. New names frequently crop up as well.

Portals

A *portal* is a good place to start when you don't know specifically what to search for. For example, when you do your initial exploration of topics that interest you, your intention is to find out what information is available on that broad subject. A portal is an ideal place to explore those general topics further. You can look at each idea to see how much information it leads to, and you may discover new ideas on which you can focus your broad topic. In other words, a portal is a type of site at which you can begin looking for any of your Internet needs. These include sites such as About.com and MSN. You use them by starting at the main site and picking your area of interest from all that are presented there.

Organizations

Research paper topics are often drawn from subjects that are closely tied to an organization of some type. Looking at the appropriate organization's Web site is then an obvious place to start. If your paper had to do with NFL football, you would start at ✑*www.nfl.com*; if your paper were related to cancer, you might start with the American Cancer Society at ✑*www.cancer.org*. Similarly, you might spend some time reading about Red Cross relief efforts at ✑*www.redcross.org* if your paper were related to their services. Once you are at the organization's site, it is much like beginning at a portal. All the related information is right there; you just need to decide where to click.

All those interesting-looking Web sites you surf by during your search can be a little too tempting. It is easy, especially if your topic is a particular passion of yours, to get sidetracked. You need to stay focused if you are going to get your research done, so try to defer visiting those interesting, but unrelated, sites you discover until after you've completed your work.

Logical Addresses

The time may come when you just can't find suitable information through any of these means. Sometimes (but not often) you can make a logical guess about the address of a potential site. (In "geek speak," an Internet address is referred to as a *URL,* which is an acronym for *uniform resource locator.*) For example, if you are looking for Web sites that have information about natural disasters, you could type in "disaster" or "tragedy." You might decide to get more specific and try different types of disasters. After a few failures you might be able to find *www.earthquakes.com,* which is the address of the Global Earthquake Response Center.

It may be helpful to note that Internet addresses commonly end with *.com,* but there are other endings. Some of the most usual are *.net,* which is used by organizations involved in Internet activities; *.org,* which is used by noncommercial organizations; and *.biz,* which is used by businesses. Internet addresses that end with only two letters are country codes—for example, *.ca* means that the site is based in Canada.

ALERT!

Typing in what you may think is a logical URL shouldn't take up too much of your time. If you come up with something reasonable within the first few tries, consider yourself lucky. But if you haven't come up with anything, give up this tactic.

When Searches Fail

Another key to using the Internet effectively is knowing how to look. The most frustrating part of Web searches can be the results you get. Sometimes they are much too general. Sometimes they return pages that are not even remotely related. And sometimes nothing at all is returned. It can seem that the Internet is temperamental, but it is the quality of your search technique that determines the quality of the results you get. The following sections will help you improve your searching skills.

Refine Keywords

Usually when you search for a topic, you type in the keyword or keywords that you are looking for. Your results will be best if you use specific words or phrases and if you choose wording that might be found on the page you want. For instance, if you search for *disaster crime* you might get some strange results. If you search for *post-disaster looting,* however, you are likely to get results more closely related to what you want.

Search terms can be written in uppercase or lowercase letters, and don't require proper English. In fact, common words such as "and" and "to" are ignored by most search engines. If you use more than one keyword, a search engine will search for pages containing all of those words no matter where it finds them on the page. If you want to search for those keywords as a complete phrase, put quotation marks around them. Therefore, using the preceding example, you would type "post-disaster looting," including the quotation marks.

One important skill to learn for your searches is how to use Boolean search terms. The word comes from the creator of such searches, mathematician George Boole. Boolean searches contain one or more of the terms "and," "or," and "not," which are called *operators*. For example, if you use the term "and" in your keywords, the search engine will retrieve results containing all of the words you entered. Enter "disaster AND looting," for instance, to retrieve results that contain both terms. Similarly, use "OR" to retrieve results that contain either term. This will be a much larger set of results. As you might guess, you use "NOT" to exclude any terms after that operator. For example, "looting NOT murder" would return results containing "looting" but not "murder." Check your search engine's FAQs (frequently asked questions) for advanced tips on using Boolean search terms.

QUESTION?

What if the word "the" is essential to my search?
If you need to include "the" or any other common words in your search, add a plus sign (+) in front of it. Make sure there is a blank space before the plus sign if another word precedes it.

Broaden or Narrow Your Search

If your search doesn't return anything useful, or anything at all, you need to broaden your search terms. Such can be the case if you search for "1942 hurricanes in new york." The results page you get tells you that your search terms didn't match any documents. If you broaden the search to "1942 hurricanes," however, many results come up. Unfortunately, many of them are references to British warplanes.

FACT

The most common error made when searching is a typo. You can't expect a search engine to give you relevant results if you type in "earthquack" instead of "earthquake" (although many search engines are smart enough to automatically correct simple typos and return results anyway). Unfortunately, search engines always look for what you type instead of what you think you type.

Sometimes your search can retrieve tens of thousands of results, or even more. This isn't much of a problem if the first page of results gives you what you want to know, but it is definitely an issue if the results have little to do with your topic. A search for "disasters" retrieves more than 2 million pages. Though the first page does have some information about airline disasters and oil spills, it contains nothing about the types of disasters you are interested in for your project. If you narrow down that search to "natural disasters," the results are reduced to just under 800 pages. Though this is still a lot, most of those on the first page are highly relevant and may be all that you need, so the large numbers of results may not be an issue. You can narrow down the results still further, but you might be wise to first take notes from what you've already found.

Where to Ask Questions Online

Aside from allowing access to Web sites, the Internet offers numerous opportunities to ask questions of anybody, living anywhere. Use caution here. Make sure the answers you receive are reliable. Just because someone answers your question doesn't automatically mean that the answer is correct.

Homework Help Sites

A homework help site at first seems like an obvious place to ask your questions. However, the probability of finding someone who can answer your questions correctly depends on your subject matter. It is one thing to visit a homework help site to ask for help with solving your calculus problem. It is quite another to visit the same site looking for reasons for a recent increase in hurricane activity. That goes beyond the realm of a typical homework help site. If you do have a question that you think is worth asking at this type of site, it is best to visit one staffed by teachers or professors.

ALERT!

Proper "netiquette" includes always thanking the people who take the time to answer your questions. Do not hound them if you don't get a response right away. They are doing you a favor in helping you out. If you need an answer within a short period of time, it is acceptable to state that deadline when you ask your question.

When asking your questions, be specific. Ask for the exact type of information you want. It is not enough to say "I would like to get more information about how tornadoes form." Instead you should say "I have researched the formation of tornadoes and there are a few factors I don't understand. All the information I have found shows a wind from the southeast near ground level and a wind from the west higher above ground. Is that the only wind direction that will result in a tornado? Why?" The experts staffing the homework help site are much more likely to answer the question phrased the second way. It asks a specific question, so they know exactly what you need answered. The first question basically asks them to tell you everything there is to know about tornadoes. The second question also shows that you have done whatever work you can on your own. You are not looking for an easy way out by having someone else answer your questions for you.

Topical Sites

Possibly your best bet for asking questions is a site that is devoted to the topic you are researching, and staffed by experts in that topic. These sites don't generally advertise that they are there to answer your questions, but they often give you the most thorough answers. They know their topic, which incidentally is also your topic, inside and out. They often have built careers around their topic. At the very least they regularly pursue hobbies related to this topic. You may have to look around such a Web site before you find an e-mail address, but most sites have it listed somewhere. It usually is a link at the bottom of the page or to one side and is listed as something like "e-mail me" or "contact us."

Newsgroups

Newsgroups, also called *Usenet,* are not as popular as they were a few years ago, but they still exist and still attract their share of enthusiasts. These enthusiasts welcome questions. Newsgroups function similarly to a bulletin board or discussion group and cover a huge range of topics. The easiest way to find a newsgroup related to your topic is to use a search engine. Google Groups, which you can access from the main Google page, has an extensive list of thousands of newsgroups, organized into general categories. The most popular newsgroup categories include these categories, which are indicated by various prefixes:

- alt.—any topic
- biz.—business products and services
- comp.—hardware and software
- humanities.—fine art and literature
- misc.—employment and health
- news.—news
- rec.—games, hobbies, and sports
- sci.—applied science and social science
- soc.—social issues and culture
- talk.—current issues and debates

Verifying What You Find

With all that information floating around the Internet, how do you know whether what you find is true or correct? You don't, actually, so you need to make sure that you always verify information that you find on the Net. This is true whether you read the information on a Web site or ask a question on a newsgroup or receive an answer via e-mail. Verify information by searching other sites or sources that you know to be reputable. If you can't confirm that the information is accurate, don't use it in your research paper.

Unfortunately, the Internet is riddled with inaccuracies. Some of us would like to believe it is because well-meaning people made mistakes when they posted the information. Some school projects are posted on the Internet without first being marked and corrected, which adds to the confusion. In reality, it is likely that some people are quite happy to post information they know is wrong.

You can avoid taking notes from inaccurate Web sites by carefully considering who published the site. Is it a professional organization or an individual? Is it part of a larger group of sites run by a company or university, or does it stand alone? Is it full of glaring grammatical and spelling errors? This is a sure sign that the site does not come from a professional.

Web sites are frequently left unattended when the owners tire of updating them. Check to see if there is a date on the page somewhere that states when the site was last updated. Some types of information will never be out of date, but other types need to be current to be useful.

This is not to say that individuals and hobbyists are responsible for all the inaccuracies and untruths found on the Internet. It also doesn't mean that some individuals and hobbyists don't put up interesting and accurate pages. It is simply a caution to double-check the accuracy of all information you find on the Internet.

Don't make the mistake of assuming that information is correct because you find it on more than one site. Erroneous information spreads like gossip, especially on the Internet.

Bookmarking Pages

Ideally, once you find a site that suits your needs, you start taking notes from it right then and there. Sometimes, however, you may only find what you are looking for after a long period of searching. But whether or not you get the notes recorded right away, it is important to bookmark the page so that you can easily return to it later. Depending on the browser you use, you usually can do this by clicking on "Favorites" in the toolbar, and then clicking on "Add."

The easiest way to organize all of your bookmarked pages for your research paper is to set up a new folder. Once you have clicked on "Add," click on the "New Folder" tab and type in a descriptive name for your folder. This way all your research sites will be kept separate from whatever else you have bookmarked.

If you are working on a school or library computer, it is probably not practical or possible to bookmark the site. In this case you can print the pages, save them into a word processing program such as Microsoft Word, or e-mail the information to yourself. In the latter two cases, make sure you include the complete address of the site.

There are several reasons for bookmarking your page. You may run out of time while taking your notes and need to return to the page later. You may find you missed something the first time around that you need to go back for. You wouldn't want to have to search for that specific page all over again. You also may discover that you forgot to add that site to your bibliography when you accessed it, so you will need to go back and take the required information from the page.

Academic Sites

With the proliferation of inaccurate Web sites, some instructors have set guidelines for the types of sites that are appropriate to use. Many instructors request that their students only use information from ".edu" sites, because those are the ones that are most dependable. Some instructors limit the use of information from any personal Web sites or from specific domains that are a little less reputable than are others. Though these guidelines may have some logic behind them, their suitability depends somewhat on the topic you are researching.

ALERT!

Web sites sometimes come and go faster than you can take notes. They may move to a new address (with or without a redirection link) or they may just disappear. Remember to take notes and record all bibliographic information on your first visit to the site in case it is gone when you try to return.

Academic Web sites can be more difficult to find. They often don't cater to the search engines and are therefore not listed in them. These are the same types of sites a librarian uses to dig up resources. They also may be sites administered by various universities and colleges. These are a few good listings of pages with links to sites that should fulfill the criteria of an academic Web site:

- O'Keefe Library's Best Information on the Net—*http://library.sau. edu/bestinfo/*
- Librarians' Index to the Internet—*http://lii.org*
- The Invisible Web Directory—*http://invisible-web.net/*
- AllLearn—*www.alllearn.org/er/directories.cgi*
- Internet Public Library—*www.ipl.org*—includes links to some academic sites

Academic Web sites differ from other Web sites mainly in the source of their information. Academic sites usually are associated with postsecondary educational institutions, and the information contained on them comes from the instructors and professors there. It is therefore very reliable information. The subject matter covers the range of topics usually learned in that institution's environment. Academic Web sites tend to be less visual and more textual than are other Web sites, although you can find many exceptions to this generalization.

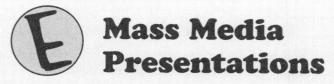

Chapter 9

Mass Media Presentations

Mass media programs are an often overlooked but interesting and frequently useful research medium. They appeal to the visual and auditory senses and allow you to see and hear about your topic, which can enable you to understand things in a different manner than just reading about your topic does. Luckily these mass media programs are quite accessible to most students. Some require another visit to the library, but you can access others from your home.

Films

Informational films that could be applicable to your research topic are similar to nonfiction books. There are films for a wealth of topics—you only need to figure out how to find them. Begin with your library's reference librarian for assistance. You may have no idea whether your library has a relevant film, or how to find it in the library, but the reference librarian can tell you if anything is available. Libraries, especially college and university libraries, generally have a number of films available. These are often in a 16 mm format, so you may have to view them while at the library.

Documentaries

A documentary is a nonfiction film that uses actual people, rather than actors playing parts, to describe the facts about a person, an event, or an issue. A multitude of different individuals and organizations produce these films. A documentary film about a person is comparable to reading a biography, because it too follows someone's life and the important things that he or she did. A documentary film about an event presents information in chronological order. Such a documentary is sometimes filmed in real time during the event, or sometimes filmed after the fact, based on personal narratives and/or other historical data. A documentary about an issue covers the people and places affected by the issue as it develops. Documentaries work well as a research source because they follow a story from beginning to end and disclose a wide range of information about the topic.

FACT

There are a variety of film catalogs that list films that have been produced and are usually available for use at a library. Each catalog specializes in a different genre or a different era or a different country. The catalog listings include a summary of each film and any related historical information. They may also include the names of the writer, director, and actors.

Promotional Films

Promotional films are those put out by companies or organizations about a product or a cause. Their purpose is to inform the public and also to encourage people to buy something or to contribute money. Though these aren't educational films, they still contain a lot of information that could be useful to you, depending on your topic. You may find such films at a library, but are more likely to have to contact whoever made the film you need. The company that produces a product would probably have a promotional film about that product. For instance, if a company came out with a new product for cleaning up oil spills in the ocean, it might produce a promotional film to send to any groups who were potential purchasers of their product. If your research paper topic were "Exploring New Methods for Cleaning Up Oil Spills," that company's film would be of interest to you. A promotional film about a cause would be made by the organization that supports the cause or informs the public about it. For example, an organization raising funds for relief of world hunger may come out with a film showing people in poverty-stricken areas that have no food. If the topic of your research paper were "Humanitarian Relief Doesn't Go to Those Who Need It," you would benefit from the things you would learn watching that promotional film.

Because these films are promotional in nature, you need to be able to distinguish between factual information and persuasive sales pitch. Consider the information in these sources carefully and follow up any facts that don't seem to be credible. These films are produced with the goal of making money from them.

Educational Films

Schools and universities use educational films to teach their students about a particular topic. These films cover a wide range of topics that are taught as part of the curriculum. They are not produced to express any opinions; they present only facts (although you should be alert to any obvious biases). Educational films are used to teach a new skill or to support one already learned, or to present information on a topic, such as a country, animal, phenomenon, and so on. They are sometimes popular with instructors because many students learn better by seeing things in addition to hearing about them. Films are particularly effective when they are used to back up or reinforce written material. The best way to find this type of film is to contact a school board or a university directly rather than going through its library.

ALERT!

Be sure to only use a fictional movie as a research source if it truly adds to your research. Adding details that are outside the scope of your topic is unnecessary and leaves the resulting paper cluttered.

Movies

Fictional movies also can be used for research in some cases. Whether or not this is the case for your project is very dependent on your topic. Even a fictional movie based on real-life circumstances needs to be used with care. Because they are produced to entertain, rather than to inform, movies usually take liberties with the facts, so you cannot use them as a factual representation of an event or a person or an issue.

Movies Related to Your Topic

In some cases a movie that's related to your topic can be a good source of research information. For example, movies about a particular time period, while not always historically accurate, can portray the general feelings and attitudes common to that period. You can see, for instance, the role of women in society or the attitudes toward people of other races in a movie depicting life in the 1950s. Sometimes the relationship between your topic and a movie is fairly vague. Suppose you were doing a research paper about survivors of leukemia. You could watch movies containing characters with leukemia to discover how the disease is perceived and how people might react to learning they have the disease. Any facts you gather from a fictional movie should be checked against a more factual source. Truths can be bent to suit the movie, so they are not reliable as a source of data.

Old or Classic Movies

Old or classic movies often can be a reliable source of research. You may use them to help you understand the feelings and attitudes of a particular period in time or to learn more about the historical aspects of the location where a movie was shot. You might also use movies as a source if your paper topic has to do with a specific actor. You could learn about the tools or household conveniences of a certain time period by watching a movie that was produced then, as long as the movie is an accurate portrayal. A classic movie that was contemporary when it was filmed is most likely to be accurate. Again, before you obtain such a movie, be sure that watching it is going to be useful to your research and not just an enjoyable waste of time.

Videos/DVDs

Videos, and more recently DVDs, are replacing other film mediums. They are better candidates as research tools because they are easier to obtain and are typically of better quality. Ideally, you should figure out first which videos you would like to see, and then find out where you can borrow or rent them.

In addition to videos that have only a peripheral relationship to your research paper, you can find videos providing instruction on how to do just about anything. These videos are meant to provide step-by-step guidance in a visual fashion, and they can be useful to you because they follow a sequence of how a particular task should be accomplished. If your project is somehow related to that task, you'll be able to see all the steps in the video. In addition to checking at the library, you could look at home improvement centers, hardware stores, or any other appropriate place that encourages a do-it-yourself approach. These places are likely to stock how-to videos as instruction for those who want to follow that approach.

Although you probably associate them with commercial films, video stores are also a viable source of other types of movies that could help you in your research. In addition to the big retail outfits, try the independent and "cult" video stores for offbeat movies. Another option is the library. Most libraries carry an ever-increasing number of videos and DVDs. In fact, most libraries carry more movies in this format than in any other format. Videos are cataloged in the library in the same way that books are. Videos usually are listed separately from books, but sometimes they're together. In the latter case, the listing will note which are books and which are videos. Your school or university may also have some videos that you can borrow, and it probably has a network of borrowing privileges with other institutions, from which you may be able to locate a video related to your topic.

FACT

Old filmstrips and photo collections are sometimes converted to video and DVD. This helps preserve what otherwise may not have lasted. This type of video or DVD could be a wonderful source of information for historical topics, as long as the conversion was done properly.

Television

Though we usually think of television as being something we watch for amusement, it can in fact be used for research, including shows that are strictly entertainment and those that are factual. The greatest benefit of using television for research is that some of the shows are live, or at least very recent. Cable television in particular offers a wide variety of channels devoted to various subjects, some of which may be related to your topic.

News and Newsmagazines

Television news is a prime example of a program that provides live information. Many channels offer news programming three or four times daily, while some, such as CNN, are news channels with continuous coverage of what is going on in the world. In addition, many networks air programs known as *newsmagazines*, such as *20/20* and *60 Minutes*, which cover timely issues, often of a controversial nature. These programs, past or present, may be helpful as you gather information.

Make sure you can differentiate between the facts presented on the news and the opinions presented on newsmagazines. Some programming may contain both facts and opinions. Sometimes the distinction between the two is so blurred that you cannot tell if you are hearing actual facts or someone's interpretation of those facts.

Newsmagazines look at news stories in depth, and often cover intriguing and unusual stories that are not covered or covered only superficially in a regular news broadcast. Newsmagazines actually discuss topics that are extremely similar in nature to research paper topics. They focus on a narrowed topic and probe into the details behind the story, including opinions and perceptions about the events. If a newsmagazine is doing a story similar to the topic of your research paper, you may very well find that the story contains a lot of useful information.

QUESTION?

Do television stations have complete transcripts or recordings of events that were only partly broadcast on the news?
Most do, but they are available on a case-by-case basis. A television news broadcast might show only the highlights from a speech due to time constraints. The television station would still have the recording of the speech in its entirety, but it may not be available to the public and it may not be transcribed.

Other Television Shows

Other television shows may be of use to you in the way that movies were useful. They might not be directly related to your topic, but may contain some relevant material. Be sure to check all the channels available in your area. If you don't get them all, find out where you could watch the others. Cable channels are likely candidates as sources for useful information because they focus on specialized areas, such as biography, sports, or medicine. Once you have watched a television show that is relevant to your project, you might want a more permanent record of the show so that you can record some notes. If you write or phone the television network, it may send you a *transcript* of the show, which is a written documentation of everything that was said. You also can request a transcript for shows you were unable to watch, which is helpful if you know that a particular program you missed was applicable to your topic. Although a few of these are provided free of charge, most networks ask for a small fee, usually based on the length of the program.

Radio

Radio is another medium that tends to be forgotten as a research source. We think of radio as something that plays music and gives brief news and weather broadcasts. Many stations offer much more, however, and some offer only alternative programming. Radio also is a very current medium, because there is no lag time before information is published, as there is with printed material. You also can purchase recordings of historical or old-time radio broadcasts. These recordings, which are available on cassette tape or CD, are sometimes rebroadcast on the radio as well.

Interviews

Interviews are a common feature of radio broadcasts. People from all walks of life—celebrities, businesspeople, local personalities, intriguing international figures—are interviewed on the radio. They are interviewed on topics as diverse as those that research papers are based on. Quite often, radio interviews are timed to promote an event or a business opening. They also may be timed to deal with a hot issue or controversy. Just as with television, you may be able to obtain transcripts of radio interviews from the station that broadcast them.

FACT

Some radio station Web sites post transcripts from the interviews they have broadcast. They also sometimes post an audio recording of the interview. That way, you can listen to it again if you missed any part, or you can go through the archives and listen to those you hadn't heard before.

Talk Radio

Some radio stations are strictly a talk format. That means that their entire programming is based on news, interviews, phone-in programs, and debates. A lot of personal opinions are aired on talk radio, but that is what you want if you are researching a controversial topic for which you need to find out the opinions of others. Talk radio is often heard on public radio stations and almost always on an AM frequency. Public radio stations, like public TV, are funded by listener donations rather than advertising. The result is that you hear only the talk radio programming, not ads. Satellite radio, such as XM Radio, is another great source of commercial-free broadcasting that includes talk shows.

You may find that none of these mass media programs suits your research topic. It is certainly not necessary to use these as sources. By now you should have plenty of information from other sources. However, if you still have insufficient information or if you find that these sources are a great fit with your topic, you should use them.

How to Search Radio Programming

Finding radio programming does not have to be hit and miss. There are ways to find out ahead of time what programs you will hear on what radio stations. Most radio stations, even the small ones, now have Web sites. These sites commonly show a schedule of programs, and list up-to-date details of the topic to be covered on each program. They also list any interviews or special guests they plan to have.

Sound Recordings

A few other audio resources may aid in your research. You can easily locate most of these with help from the reference librarian or staff in the audio/ video section of the library. The recordings are usually listed separately in the library catalog.

Speeches

Listening to a speech related to your topic is a powerful way to bring the words to life for you. Suppose your topic included a reference to Martin Luther King Jr.'s "I Have a Dream" speech. Do you think it would mean more to you to read a transcript of the speech or to hear him speaking on tape?

A speech you listen to brings out the inflections in a voice and the timing in the presentation, which can make a big difference in your understanding of the speech. The crowd's reaction also can greatly aid your understanding of what the public's response was at the time. Depending on the format in which a speech is stored, you may be able to sign it out or may have to listen to it in the library.

It is helpful to have the transcript as well as the audio recording of a speech. Sometimes it is difficult to make out exactly what the speaker is saying. It's also possible that you may think you hear the speech correctly but misinterpret the words. If you can follow along on the transcript while you listen, there is no room for error.

Music

Music resources include all styles of music found on DVD, CD, cassette tape, and older formats. You can sign out the music in the newer formats from a library, but because it is unlikely that you have the equipment to listen to the older formats, such as a turntable to listen to LP records, you probably will have to listen to these at the library. You might want to listen to numerous recordings of the same piece of music to compare their styles and interpretation, or to music from a different country or a piece that was written for a unique instrument.

Chapter 10

Museums and Historical Sites

Many students choose to write their research papers about a historical figure or an issue of historical significance. They write about topics that deal with a specific location or an event with ties to history. Even if your topic is not historical in nature, looking into the past can add to the information that you present in your paper. You may find crucial background information that leads up to the events in question, or explore the lives of the people central to your research paper topic.

What You Can Discover

This may be the first time you have ever visited a museum or a historical site as part of the research process. In fact, these may seem like strange places to be doing research. There are no large volumes of reference information, no computers, and they are places you are probably more familiar with from visiting as a tourist, not as a student. You may be surprised at just how much you can discover at a museum or historical site.

Photographs

Historical photos have many uses. Such photos are a visual record of places, events, and people. A photo of a specific location in a certain year is a graphic record of landforms, vegetation, and buildings that often no longer exist. Photos were often taken, as they are now, to commemorate an event. Photos would have been taken at a presidential inauguration or at the completion of building a railway. Though most photos were staged, as opposed to being candid, they still represent the key people involved at the time. Whenever it is known, historical photographs will include the date and location of the photo and the names of all those shown. Looking at historical photos can reveal any of the following:

- People who were present at a particular event
- Clothing worn by people in a certain time period
- Tools and machinery used by people in a certain time period
- Family and friends of a historical figure
- How specific locations have changed in appearance over time

Larger museums often have gift shops that sell reproductions of the art and photography contained in their collections. If you're very lucky, you may be able to purchase a postcard or other replica of the image you want to include in your research paper.

You will not be able to include original photos in your research paper if they only exist as part of a display. If that's the case, you can describe what you see in the photo in detail, or jot down particular features you note and where you saw them. You need to take these notes at the time you see the photo; do not try to write them later from memory.

Letters and Journals

Handwritten records are another extremely useful form of research material. Family members who understand the significance of these objects often donate them to a museum. Because they are penned during the writer's life throughout a certain period in history, they represent a first-person account of the events and the feelings of the time. They often are written on a very personal level, with no details left out. Letters of interest could be those written home to a loved one or those written to a colleague. Journals, or diaries, are written on an even more personal level. They chronicle the writer's most intimate thoughts and knowledge and thus can sometimes dispel commonly held beliefs. Letters and journals may be written during a war or during a journey to a new place. They may be written by honorable citizens or by hardened criminals, and by people of any age, race, or social background. Because of this diversity, letters and journals cover a wide range of topics, and you can draw a wide range of information from them. Although the original copies of these letters and journals are too fragile to be handled, some have been turned into books. While these are occasionally edited to some extent, they still contain much of the author's original writing. These include such works as the following:

- *Anne Frank: The Diary of a Young Girl*—Anne Frank was a teenaged Jewish girl in hiding from the Nazis with her family. The events that she wrote about occurred in Amsterdam from 1942 to 1944.
- *The Diary of Samuel Pepys*—Written from 1660 to 1669 in London, England, Samuel Pepys's diary includes his thoughts about the Great Plague and the Great Fire of London.
- *Lincoln's Letters*—This is a collection of letters and speeches written by Abraham Lincoln. They are arranged in chronological order.
- *Florence Nightingale's Theology*—These are the essays, letters, and

journal notes of the woman who is regarded as the founder of nursing as we know it.

- *Diary of a Confederate Soldier*—These are the memoirs of John S. Jackman of the Civil War's Orphan Brigade.

Another possible source for these materials is audiobooks, which are an excellent option for students (or anyone) with a long commute.

ALERT!

Because letters and journals are writings of a personal nature, instead of hard data, they may contain misleading information. However, they do offer insight into personal feelings that hard data does not reveal, and questionable information can be compared to other recognized sources of information.

Documents

Historical documents include all other written records that are not personal writing. These could include land titles; records of immigration, marriage, birth, and death; passenger lists for ships or trains; or court records. This is only a small sampling of the type of documents you may find at a museum or historical site. What you actually find depends both on your research paper topic and on the availability of certain historical documents. It also depends on the type of museum or historical site you visit. One that is specialized has documents relating to that specialized topic. Of course, you want to make use of every piece of data and every record you can find that fits in with your topic. But at times it is not immediately evident that the information contained in a document is of use to you. It is usually best to record everything you find that might be useful, and go through your notes later to decide whether in fact your research paper benefits from that information.

For example, suppose you are writing a paper about the Underground Railway. You are following the story of a certain slave who escaped to freedom. You may be looking for a record of which ship brought this man to America, the date and place he died, and any land titles he held after he was freed, but you also may find bank records, military records, or baptismal records at a museum or historical site along the slave route he traveled. You also may find these documents at a site specifically dedicated to the issue, such as the National Underground Railroad Freedom Center in Cincinnati, Ohio.

Data from historical documents must be copied down exactly. Always double-check to be sure that you have recorded correct dates, names, and places, including correct spelling. If you find two records that don't agree, seek out another source to confirm which is correct. If you cannot find another record, write down the information from both sources.

Museums

Almost every town has a museum of some sort. Larger centers may have several. Some of these are general or historical museums; others are specialized museums that focus on a particular interest, such as aviation, art, dolls, or a specific culture. Don't assume that all museums house only things from the past.

ALERT!

You usually can't take any information home from a museum. All your research work must be done on-site. You need to take meticulous notes of all pertinent information, accurately write down dates and names, and summarize or quote directly from written documents. There may be the odd exception to this rule, but in general, museum materials stay where they are.

Exhibits

One thing common to all types and sizes of museums is that every exhibit is well documented. They all are clearly labeled, and many have accompanying information. Well-funded exhibits also frequently sell glossy catalogs or books about the items. Traveling, or temporary, exhibits are based on a certain theme and may contain newly discovered or donated items. These traveling exhibits are owned by other museums or private donors, who circulate the exhibit to other museums. Before you visit a museum, it is a good idea to find out a bit about what to expect there. Many museums have a Web site you can visit for information about permanent and temporary exhibits. If you can easily reach a museum that specializes in an area related to your topic, find out whether the museum has a mailing list to which you can be added. When you learn about an exhibit that interests you, try to visit the museum on a weekday, when it may be less crowded. You also can phone the museum before you visit to ask specific questions, and the staff may even arrange to have someone help you find what you want when you come to visit.

Curator Help

The curator is the director of a museum and overlooks all aspects of its operation. Because of the curator's expertise, it only makes sense that you approach him or her for help just as you would a librarian. The curator can tell you what is available in the museum and where to look for specific information, and also can sometimes get things brought in from other museums for you. It is important to ask the curator for help because many museums do not display everything that they have on hand. Some objects or documents may be stored and only brought out for occasional display. The curator can locate those items for you if they are pertinent to your research paper.

Museum Photos

Different museums have different rules about allowing photography. You need to check with each museum to find out what its specific policy is. Some don't allow any cameras at all; others allow you to take pictures as long as you don't use a flash. (Flash can cause older exhibits to deteriorate.) In those museums that allow photos without flashbulbs, you may have difficulty because of the lack of lighting. Even those that do allow flash photography often house their displays behind glass, which can make it difficult to get a good shot. At some museums you will be asked to sign a permit that states, among other things, your purpose for taking photos.

Historical Sites

Historical sites are monuments, forts, and other structures and features that are generally located at the scene of a former event. Note that there are museums at many, but not all, historical sites. These sites range from a simple marker to an elaborate replica of a previous site.

QUESTION?

What should I do if the historical sites relevant to my topic are too far away to visit?
Most historical sites are happy to send you an information package to aid in your research. Write or phone to request this, and include any specific questions that you may have.

What is displayed at a historical site depends on the type of site it is. A heritage village has the village laid out as it would have looked in whatever years it is depicting. A fort rebuilt from the original is likely be in its original location. Live performers in costumes from the era may be employed there, or the site could be populated only with mannequins. Any related information, such as that found in a museum, also is on display at a historical site.

Informational pamphlets and brochures are usually available either at the site itself or from a nearby tourism office or hotel. These pamphlets provide the basic information but don't go into too much depth. They can be useful for research if you are unable to make it to the historical site itself, and may give you ideas to research further.

The staff at a historical site has been well trained in all aspects of that site. Take advantage of any tours that are offered, because some information is only shared during these tours. Be sure to ask any questions you have at any point. If the staff members don't know the answer themselves, they may know who to ask or where to look for answers.

Historical Societies

There are historical societies in many communities and in areas of any size. There also are historical societies for various ethnic groups and for special interest groups. These societies exist for the purpose of preserving and recording the history of its particular interest group. Historical societies are sometimes run in conjunction with a museum or historical site, and the larger societies sometimes have their own library.

One of the things that a historical society does is track the genealogical history of an area. The society keeps records pertaining to people who lived in a certain area or those of various groups. If your paper deals with a local historical person, whether or not he or she is well known, your local historical society may be a good place to look for information. For example, the Chicago Historical Society has a collection of information about Al Capone.

If you have a lot of questions, ask the staff after the tour. There are likely to be others on the tour who won't want their time taken up by extensive questioning that may go beyond their interest level. If staff members cannot answer your questions, they can refer you to someone else at the site who can.

Because historical societies deal with a specific place or time in the past, they could be a good source of local historical information. Their mandate may be to record information that otherwise has not been recorded elsewhere. Their members often have valuable knowledge that could help in your research. They may even have a museum-like collection of local historical information, or they may put out publications about local history.

City Hall

Your city or town hall is probably full of records that you can use in your research. Often there is a fee for retrieving the information, and in some cases a search may take a long time. Make sure you know up front how much it will cost and how long it will take to get the information so you can decide if it is worthwhile.

All types of vital records of a city's population are usually retained by city hall. These include birth, death, marriage, and divorce records. There may be regulations regarding which of these records can be released to the public. It is common for records to not be released if the person in question is still living or if that person is not related to you at all. City hall may also have records of court cases, census data, and directories showing home-owners' occupations.

Property records are also usually retained by city hall. These records show owners of all properties within the city, and dates of ownership. They may show property tax information. Some city halls may also have more obscure information. For instance, during 1939 and 1940, every house in New York City was photographed for the purpose of property tax assess-ment. Anyone can see these photos at the municipal archives.

City hall also has records related to business activities in the city. These include business licenses, liens, building permits, and more. You also can find political records, including municipal voter registration lists, and city council documents, including minutes, ordinances, and resolutions, at your local city hall.

Other Historical Institutions

Your search for historical information can take you to still more places. Because different places vary in the type of information they hold, it is to your benefit to check out as many different resources as you can. Your research topic and your location partly determine which resources are the best for you, but the following are the most likely to be useful.

National Archives

Most countries in the world have national archives. They are similar to a library, but include all information that is directly related to that country and its history. Usually this information is in all forms that may be found in a regular library, including books, letters, legal documents, films, photos, newspapers, and works of art. The national archives are commonly found in a nation's capital city; however, most have extensive Web sites where you can access parts of the collections. The Web site for U.S. National Archives & Records Administration (NARA) is at *www.archives.gov.*

Census Records

Census records provide an abundance of information about the people in a specific region in a specific year. In some regions there may be an annual census; in others the census may only be taken in certain years. Census data is usually searched by year or by region, but it could also be searched by any other data that has been collected. This data will vary from one census to another, but it could include the following:

- Last name
- First name
- Address
- Relationship to head of household
- Sex
- Race
- Languages spoken
- Occupation
- Marital status

Immigration Records

Immigration records are helpful if you need information about a particular person or if you are researching trends in immigration. This could include trends in immigrants from a particular country or numbers of immigrants in general. These records are generally in the form of passenger lists or border entry lists, and they show the names of all immigrants, their dates of arrival in the country, and their birthplace.

Immigration records for many years can be obtained from NARA (see the National Archives section) or from the Latter Day Saints Family History Library (see next section). You will be required to fill out a formal request form, after which a staff member will complete the search for you, or you may be able to search through microfilmed records. A fee applies to some of these searches. You may also be able to find ship passenger lists online yourself; however, only a small number of these are available currently. For a successful search, you should know the full name of the person you are researching, the port at which he or she arrived, the approximate date of arrival, and the name of the ship on which the person traveled.

Family History Library

The Family History Library is another resource of data about historical people and families. Located in Salt Lake City, Utah, this huge library of genealogical data is run by The Church of Jesus Christ of Latter Day Saints. It is the largest library of its kind in the world. There are Family History Centers located in many other cities that have access to the materials from the main library, and you can also search the records from the library's Web site at *www.familysearch.org*. The Web site contains the following information:

- Birth, marriage, and death records
- Census returns
- Court, property, and probate records
- Cemetery records
- Emigration and immigration lists
- Family and county histories

FACT

The Family History Library was founded in 1894 and houses five floors of records. Most of the records are for people who lived prior to 1930. These now include more than 2.4 million rolls of microfilmed genealogical records; 742,000 microfiche; 310,000 books, serials, and other printed material; 4,500 periodicals; and 700 electronic resources.

Military Records

If you are researching a person who served in the military at some point, you can receive a copy of his or her military record. Requests for these records usually have to be made in writing using a particular form, and it may take some time to receive the record, so this should be done early in the research process. Some records are confidential, so check to ensure that there are no restrictions on the information you are seeking. Usually these records include name, dates served, medical information including injuries, and a list of any awards or medals received. They may also include medical records of military personnel after retirement from service.

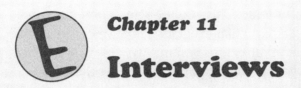

Chapter 11

Interviews

Conducting an interview can be the best way to uncover information not found elsewhere. There are many knowledgeable people who have all sorts of insight into their particular area of expertise. This insight is often not recorded in any form. In some ways you are conducting an interview every time you ask questions of a librarian or a curator or any staff you may have already come across. But there are more formal interviews that you should include as part of your research paper.

Who to Interview

Make sure that you find an interview subject who can add something to your paper. There is no point in interviewing someone just for the sake of conducting an interview. If that person cannot supply any new information to you, you are simply wasting your time. You need to find a person with inside knowledge of your topic. This could be an expert in the field, a person who was present at a particular event, or a relative or friend of someone your paper is based on. In rare cases you may be able to interview the person who is central to your research paper topic. If you are very fortunate, you may be able to conduct more than one interview, given enough time. Choosing whom to interview is just as important as asking the right questions, so be sure to think this through carefully.

Asking an Acquaintance

You may already know someone who would make an ideal interviewee. Think of your friends, relatives, neighbors, and anyone else that you know at all. Bring up your topic in conversation, and discuss the fact that you are looking for an interview subject. Many times you may already know an ideal candidate, but you may not be aware that he or she knows specific things about your topic. For instance, you may be writing a research paper on "How the 1969 Woodstock Festival Differed from Other Concerts." You might find out that your uncle attended the concert and that he is receptive to an interview. You might also talk to a friend about your paper and find out that her neighbor lived near Woodstock at the time. The neighbor also is a great interviewee, but you would never have known that if you hadn't been talking about your paper.

QUESTION?

Is there an easier way to conduct many interviews for which I'll be asking everyone the same questions?
You could use a questionnaire. These are most effective if they contain only a few questions and those questions are fairly straightforward. There should be no confusion about what you are asking in a questionnaire.

When you decide to interview an acquaintance, you need to approach that person to ask if he or she would agree to be interviewed. Briefly give your acquaintance the background of your research paper topic before you ask so that he or she will have some idea of what you will be asking about. You need to approach this with a degree of professionalism, no matter how close you are to the person. Treat the interview seriously and follow the same steps you would follow if you weren't interviewing an acquaintance.

Approaching Someone You Don't Know

You may need to approach someone you don't know for an interview. Maybe you really don't know anyone with any special knowledge of your topic, or there may be a person or a few people who obviously are the best people to interview for your paper. These may be local people, or they may be people who are a great distance from you. You can approach someone you don't know for an interview in a number of ways. You could ask in person, over the phone, or via e-mail or regular mail. In any case, begin by introducing yourself and stating the reason for contacting the person. Include any details briefly, but don't take up too much of his or her time with your request.

You do not always need to conduct interviews in person. You also can conduct them over the phone or online via e-mail or using a chat. The benefit of Internet interviews is that everything is in writing, so you don't need to do any further note taking. The downside, though, is that they are not as spontaneous—answers are often thought out and edited, so interesting details may be omitted.

If you are able to interview more than one person, leave the most important or influential person until last. By this time you will have gained insight from all the other interviews that may bring up some interesting questions. You will also have learned all the background information from the previous interviews, and will no doubt have honed your interviewing skills.

Reluctant Interviewees

Ideally, you will have success in your requests for interviews. However, you may come across some people who are reluctant to agree to an interview. This is especially the case if you want to talk to them about a sensitive issue or one that will expose a secret. In this instance you have a few options. You may be more comfortable with dropping them as potential interviewees and asking someone else. If you know of other people who could offer similar information, this may be the best route to take. If not, you may want to try to convince reluctant interviewees that agreeing to an interview with you will not place them in jeopardy. You could offer to give them a list of your questions beforehand so they can think their answers through, or give them the option to not answer any questions that make them uncomfortable. Both of these suggestions will leave you with less information, but they may be worthwhile if this is the only way you can get anything from an interview.

Preparing for an Interview

Preparation is the most important part of the interview. This is not an exercise you can go into without a plan. If you are not fully ready for an interview, you will waste both your time and that of your interviewee. You should not approach this as if it is a casual conversation. Be ready for a professional consultation.

FACT

All interviews should have a purpose. There should be something in particular that you are trying to learn from the interview. Keep this purpose in mind as you formulate potential questions, and remember this purpose during the interview if it starts to go off track.

Make an Appointment

Once you have a subject who has agreed to the interview, you need to make an appointment with him or her. It is vital to set aside a day, time, and place that will give you the best results. Don't choose the same day that you make your initial contact, even if the interviewee is available. You want to give yourself time to prepare for the interview. You also want to conduct the interview with no interruptions or distractions, and to do it where both the questions and the answers can be heard clearly to avoid any confusion. Sometimes it is a good idea to meet in a neutral, public place to conduct the interview. That way, you are less likely to be interrupted by ringing telephones or other family members. Of course, you should always honor the preferences of the person you are interviewing. If the person you ask to interview wants you to ask your questions on the spot, be firm in requesting an appointment. Most of the time you will request an in-person interview, but be open to the subject's suggestions for an interview over the phone or by e-mail.

Once you have an appointment, it is essential that you be punctual. Be there on time, in the right place, and with all the materials you need to conduct your interview. Decide ahead of time how long your interview should take, and let the interviewee know the approximate length of time you are asking for. Be careful not to exceed this time limit by any more than a few minutes, unless the interviewee is clearly enjoying the opportunity to share the information and doesn't mind spending the extra time.

Be accurate in your estimation of the time your interview should take. While it is impossible to know how long the interviewee will take in answering your questions, you do know ahead of time what you want to find out. Keep an eye on the time to make sure you cover the most important areas.

Background Information

One of the things you can do to get ready for the interview is to collect background information about the person you will be talking to. You will have already done a lot of research into your topic, but you may not have many details about how this person relates to your topic. Before the interview, try to find out a bit about the interviewee's experience. The type of experience could include his or her relationship with a person, involvement in an event, or employment background. You will touch on some of this information again in your interview, but if you know some of it before the interview, you can figure out where you want the questioning to take you.

Prepare Questions

Perhaps the most important thing you can do prior to the interview is to prepare questions to ask. This is not a rigid list of every question you will ask in the interview, because interviews can take a direction of their own once they get going. But you should have an idea beforehand of what you want to learn from the interview. Draft a list of possible questions, knowing that you will probably ask others that aren't on the list and omit some that are. It is awkward to begin an interview with no idea of what questions to ask.

Questions to Ask

When you conduct an interview, you need to make the most of your time. The purpose of the interview is to add to the other information you have found through your research. You might find it easiest to brainstorm for all the potential questions you can think of, and then cross off or reword the ones you don't think are pertinent.

Obtain New Information

You conduct an interview to learn details that you didn't find in your previous research. It is pointless to hear responses that are just a repetition of what you have read or seen elsewhere. As your research progresses, you probably can identify some gaps in the information, such as insights that data couldn't provide but that personal experience does. The perceptions of your interview subject should tell you what you couldn't find elsewhere, but you'll have to ask the right questions to find out what that person's perceptions are.

Thinking on the Spot

Though it is essential to prepare questions ahead of time, those questions may change completely over the course of the interview. You may hear answers that take you by surprise. These answers could lead the interview in a different direction than you expected. You may find that what you thought you would hear is different from what you are hearing. For example, you may be interviewing a former employee of an oil company about a spill the company had. You may expect the employee to tell you that it was simply an accident or the result of an error in judgment. Instead, she tells you that these spills happen all the time and are usually covered up by management. You would want to change your line of questioning at that point to find out the whole story. No amount of forethought could have prepared you for this revelation.

It is important to think quickly while you are conducting the interview. Be prepared to ask totally different questions than those you had planned if anything interesting comes up. You may also find that your interviewee doesn't want to answer a certain line of questioning or that the person doesn't know some of the details you had assumed that he or she would. Be prepared to alter your line of questioning, and don't be shy about asking for leads to other potential interviewees.

Getting People to Talk

Some people love to talk and will give you detailed answers to every question you ask. Your only problem with them may be to keep them on topic and to get all your questions answered in the amount of time you have allowed for the interview. Other people will state their answers to your questions as briefly and succinctly as possible. Your challenge then is to get them to elaborate on their responses.

Some interviewees prefer to remain anonymous. As long as the person is credible, and assuming that you don't have any other possible interviewees who could give you the same or similar information, you should honor this request. In your report, you need to identify such interviewees while preserving their anonymity. Examples might include "a prominent local business leader" or "a national baseball player."

The way you word your questions can make a big difference in the way they are answered. Some questions will just be about facts, and these are generally answered briefly. But you should also ask about the interviewee's feelings or ask for a description of events, and these answers will be much longer. You should ask open-ended questions—that is, those that allow for a detailed answer as opposed to a "yes" or a "no." Make sure your questions don't show your own opinion on an issue, because you don't want to influence the answers or offend the person you are interviewing. For example, if you were interviewing a local politician, such as a city council member, about a proposed dog control bylaw concerning dangerous dogs, you might ask these questions:

- What exactly is a dangerous dog?
- What additional things would the owners of dangerous dogs have to do in regard to licensing, muzzles, and so on if this new bylaw is adopted?
- What breeds of dogs do you consider to be more dangerous than others?
- Why doesn't the city think it should ban certain breeds of dogs?
- Some dogs are a continual threat to those in their neighborhoods. What is proposed in this bylaw for owners who won't keep those dogs under control?

There may be times when a response makes you suddenly think of a further question. Resist the urge to interrupt, which disrupts the answer the person was already giving. Jot down a word or two to ensure that you remember to ask the new question after the current question has been answered.

ALERT!

The interviewee may have questions to ask you at this time. This is fine as long as you are comfortable with them. The interviewee may also be able to offer further details that you missed asking about. Because this person is central to the topic, these details almost always are a welcome addition to your project.

Follow-up Questions

Once you finish asking the questions you prepared in advance and asking those you thought of during the interview, you are almost finished. But before you conclude your interview, you need to follow up. Not only might the interviewee have some information to add, but you may also find holes in what you have learned.

Questions That Weren't Fully Answered

You may find that some questions you asked were only partially answered. This is sometimes the case when you ask two questions at the same time. Suppose you asked, "Where were you working at the time, and is that where you met Mr. Smith?" The interviewee may have responded with a lengthy description of the job he or she held at the time and may even have talked about working with Mr. Smith on that job, but may not have really said whether that is where they met or whether they had known each other previously. Make sure you have full answers to all the questions you still think are important before you leave the interview.

Answers You Don't Understand

You should also make sure that you understand all the answers you are given. Some answers may include technical details that are beyond your comprehension. Others may just not be logical, or years and locations and other details from multiple questions may not make sense. Now is the time to clarify answers rather than trying to sort them out later. Ask the interviewee if there is anything to add, or if there was something he or she was hoping you would ask. It is also fine to ask interviewees if they mind being contacted once more for clarification of anything said during the interview.

Always remember to thank interview subjects for their time. They have gone out of their way to donate time and information to help with your research paper. Handwritten thank-you notes are best, and it's always nice to send a copy of your final paper to each interviewee.

Taping Versus Taking Notes

You need to record an oral interview in some manner. You should never rely on your memory for any part of an interview no matter how short or how general the interview it is. You can record the interview yourself, or you can have someone come with you to do the recording. Bringing someone with you should be cleared with the interviewee ahead of time. You should also get his or her consent for whatever form of recording you choose to do, even though interviewees usually expect to be recorded.

Pros and Cons of Taping

You may choose to use a tape recorder for your interview. This allows you to keep your mind on the interview, moving forward rather than trying to keep up with what was already said. If you need to clarify anything that was said, you could go back and listen to it over again. Because you have the interviewee's voice on tape, you have irrefutable proof of what he or she said. Capturing his or her voice also enables you to listen again for its tone, and you can often pick up feelings of nervousness, hesitation, or excitement that you may have missed the first time around.

However, taping has its drawbacks unless you have a newer digital voice recorder. Tape recorders can malfunction, batteries can run out, cassettes can break, and the volume can be too low to hear. If your interview is very long, you may run out of tape before you are done. It is very important to completely test the tape recorder before the interview, and it is often helpful to test it partway through as well. You should always bring extra batteries and extra cassettes with you, along with a notepad and pen in case the taping doesn't work out. As a precaution, always take some brief notes even if you are recording the interview.

If the interview is conducted over the phone and you are using a tape recorder, you will need to use a speakerphone. Make sure the tape recorder is positioned where it can pick up both your voice and that of your interviewee.

Pros and Cons of Taking Notes

Some people prefer to keep it simple and take notes throughout the interview. This way they can be sure that there are no technical difficulties. Notes are easy to look through at the end of the interview when you want to make certain that you didn't miss anything. They can also be easier to review when it is time to collate all your information into your research paper. Moreover, interview subjects are usually much more comfortable with notes than with a recording device.

On the other hand, when you are taking notes you put a lot of effort into writing down what is being said. Sometimes vital information is missed, and if you want to get a direct quote it can be difficult to write down every word quickly enough. You only get one chance to record the interview in your notes. At times you may need to interrupt the flow of the interview to catch up with what you are writing. Also, there is always the chance that an interviewee will dispute what you wrote down and claim that he or she said something different.

You should always go into an interview with backup material for taking notes. Bring an extra pencil or pen in case yours breaks or doesn't work, and have more paper than you think you'll use. If you are using a tape recorder, you should bring extra batteries and an extra cassette tape.

Rechecking Information

Immediately following the interview, you should reread or listen to everything that you recorded. You can add notes about anything that you perceived about the interview subject at the time, such as "He appeared tired" or "She had a large bruise on her cheek." At the same time, you may notice some information that still needs to be rechecked or clarified.

You may need to get in touch with an interviewee one more time for clarification. Make sure you gather all your interview notes before this contact. Clear up everything with one phone call, rather than contacting someone repeatedly.

You may need to use other sources to clarify things you learned in your interview. For example, the interviewee may not have been sure about a specific year. You may be able to look up this information elsewhere instead of using the vague information obtained during the interview. Only data can be clarified in this way. The thoughts and opinions of the person you talked to remain the same even if they go against those of other people.

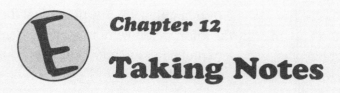

Chapter 12

Taking Notes

With all the emphasis on gathering information from unique and varied research sources, you may wonder about the specifics of how to gather those notes. Once you have located the information, what do you do with it? The key is to take notes from the information, but that is not as simple as it may sound. There is a right way and a wrong way to take notes. The right way ensures that you gather all the correct and relevant information, while the wrong way could result in a loss or misinterpretation of valuable research.

Put It in Your Own Words

Note taking is much different from copying the information you find. When you write a research paper, or any type of report, you need to gather the information, read or view it until you understand it, and then take notes from it. There is no sense in writing down what someone else wrote about the topic. When you copy directly from another source, no critical thinking is involved. It is too easy to copy the information without really understanding or thinking about what you are writing. Put the information in your own words to ensure that you fully comprehend it.

FACT

When you put notes in your own words, you are always paraphrasing and sometimes summarizing. Paraphrasing is restating information or ideas using your own words and presenting it in your own form. Summarizing is condensing a main idea into a shorter format, also in your own words.

The jury is still out regarding the best way to record and organize your notes. There are three main methods. You can use index cards or full-sized lined paper to write on, or type notes directly into your computer. The system you use depends on your personal preference; there are pros and cons to each. Some people like to use index cards, writing each note or each similar group of notes on a separate card. This can result in a large stack of index cards, but they can be easier to sort out and put in order later on. Other people prefer regular lined paper, using one page for every group of similar notes or skipping a line for a new group of ideas or information. Much more information can fit on a full piece of paper, but it can be more challenging to find a way to use this method for sorting and outlining later. If you decide to use regular sheets of paper, it is best to write on only one side of the page. That way you avoid having to flip back and forth when you use your notes to begin writing. Typing notes on the computer makes it easy to reorganize your material using the word processor's cut and paste feature.

Whatever you use to write your notes on, you may want to include information about the source directly beside the note. Use any shorthand that works for you. Just be sure that you can find the full citation later when you need to prepare the bibliography. Include a volume number or page number if applicable, which you'll need in order to recheck any information later.

ALERT!

As you progress, you may find that most of your notes fall into a few general categories. It may be helpful for your future outlining to make note of the category that would be an obvious fit for that particular note. Then when it comes time to organize your notes, you have these headings to go by.

Change the Wording Right Away

Too often students try to take shortcuts by copying information straight from the source, believing that they will put it in their own words when they write the first draft. This usually leads to writing the first draft straight from that information. It is very difficult to copy notes directly from a source and not use some of the same wording in your draft. When you write the draft from your own notes, there is no wording to influence you but your own.

You should change the wording to your own as you take notes from your research. Doing this ensures that you are not copying anything word for word, and confirms that you understand the content of those notes. Doing this won't take much more time than it does to copy things directly, and it will make the final paper much easier to write. Suppose you read this: "The ancient Incan city of Machu Picchu is thought to have once been a religious retreat. Found there is an *intihuatana*, a slab of stone where a priest would perform a ceremony as the winter solstice approached. He would try to tie the sun to the stone to keep it from disappearing." Your notes from this might be put in point form, including one point for each, such as "Machu Picchu was an Incan city"; "may have had religious significance." You would also add "they had an *intihuatana*—a big rock to which a priest tried to attach the sun symbolically when winter was coming."

Use Note Form

At this point you do not write your information into paragraphs. In fact, it's just a waste of your time if you do. Because you are gathering information from an assortment of different sources, some areas of research may be repeated. If you try to put it all in paragraph form at this time, you will end up rewriting those paragraphs once you have all the information together.

As you gather information, write it down in note form. Don't use any sentences; just write the main facts. Descriptive phrases are fine if they are literally part of the meaning, but not if they are part of the original writer's judgment. For instance, you could write that someone had a child, but not that it was "sullen and apathetic."

ALERT!

Notes make it easier to write your paper using your own words. Without someone else's phrases and sentences, you won't be tempted to write things in the same fashion they did. It also means that you can organize your paper in any order that suits you. Some information that you found together may fit better in separate places in your paper.

Keep the Meaning

Some students have difficulty writing the notes in their own words without changing the meaning. This usually occurs when they don't yet have a full understanding of what they have read. It is therefore important to make sure you completely understand what you read before you change it into your own words.

Ensure That Your Notes Make Sense

Your notes have to make sense when you come back to them to write the first draft. By the time you research all aspects of your topic and draw information out of every source you can find, weeks go by. While it may be hard to believe at the time, you might not remember a lot about those initial notes you took. When you first take the notes, reread them to be sure they make sense.

Make sure that you haven't left out anything important. This will help greatly when you look at them again and begin to put the rough draft together.

Use Information in Context

A common error in note taking is to use a phrase out of context. You must make sure that you include enough background information in your notes that they aren't misinterpreted. For example, you could be taking notes about people who die while exercising. Your notes might state that "physically fit people risk death when exercising." While this is true to some extent, the source you took it from meant that there are cases of people dying when they took part in vigorous exercise, including some who were physically fit. Without the background information, your notes could be very misleading.

Plagiarism

Plagiarism is stealing. Instead of stealing a material object, however, plagiarizing is stealing an idea. If you copy someone else's work and claim it to be your own, you are stealing that person's creation. This is true whether the work is in an encyclopedia, in a book, in a film, on the Internet, or elsewhere. Not only is it wrong, it is also illegal. There is no excuse for plagiarism at any level, but by the time you are writing research papers you must know that it is not acceptable.

You must take plagiarism very seriously. Penalties vary greatly, but they range from receiving an "F" grade on your research paper to failing that particular course to being expelled from your school or college. It is no excuse to say that you didn't realize that what you did was considered plagiarism.

What Is and Is Not Acceptable

You are probably already aware that using an entire paper is plagiarism. What you may not realize is that duplication of even a small part of a paper is also considered plagiarism. This is why it is so important to put all your notes in your own words. That gets rid of any temptation, conscious or not, to copy someone else's wording or ideas. It is actually also plagiarism to copy your own work. You cannot submit a paper you wrote for another class even if it was in a different year. Nor can you submit anything you wrote for your own Web site or for a school newspaper, because that also is still plagiarism. The only time it is acceptable to copy something directly is when you are using it as a quote, as discussed in detail in the next section. All other information and details must be written using your own words to describe them.

Quoting a Source

There are times when you want to quote a source directly. You might want to quote a person, or you might want to quote information directly from a written source. Either way, you must clearly state that the material is a quote. A complete discussion of the rules governing the treatment of quoted material is beyond the scope of this book. You can find several excellent books describing quoted material and other rules of punctuation, including *The Chicago Manual of Style* and the *Publication Manual of the American Psychological Association*. Check with your instructor first to find out whether a particular guide is preferred.

QUESTION?

Is there an easy way to remember what was taken down as a quote?
The best way is to record the citation information alongside the quote. An extra benefit to doing this is that you won't have to hunt through all of your materials for that information when you need it for your bibliography. You can always use a highlighter pen or a star to make the quotes stand out from the rest of your notes.

The basic rule is that all quotes must be enclosed in quotation marks. Any other punctuation marks are usually placed outside the quotation marks, unless they are part of the quote itself. The exceptions to this rule are the period and the comma. So you would write "The tools they were required to use were faulty." and "Does this mean that those tools are to blame for the injuries of thousands of people?" and "My colleague was quick to blame the tools but essentially it was his own fault!" If your quote contains another quote within it, the double quotation marks (") will still be used for the main quote. The quote within the quote is designated with single quotation marks. As an example, you would write "Oddly enough, he always repeated 'A little learning is a dangerous thing.' That was from Alexander Pope, and it didn't seem to be the kind of thing he believed in." The source of your quote also needs to be *cited*. This just means letting the reader know the source of your quote. There are quite a few different citation styles, so your instructor will probably tell you the requirements for citing quotes in your paper. If you are using MLA style, for instance, you would insert just the author's last name and page number where the quote was found, in parentheses, immediately following the quote. A complete citation would also appear in your bibliography.

Be sure to use quotes sparingly. Use them only when they show a particularly strong opinion, when they demonstrate an authoritative source, or when they demonstrate a colloquial way of speaking that has some significance to your topic. Avoid using quotes throughout your research paper. The paper will have much more impact if it is largely in your own words. Research paper assignments often limit the number of quotes that can be used.

You Won't Get Away with It

While it should be enough of a deterrent to know that plagiarism is wrong, you should also know that most instructors are becoming increasingly adept at detecting plagiarism. The increased use of the Internet in conducting research has led to more copied works. Many instructors know of and will check the places that sell complete research papers to see if there are any there that sound familiar. There also are special Web sites with tools that an instructor can use to detect plagiarism. The instructor inserts a phrase from a paper into the tool and it returns a list of Web pages containing that phrase. The instructor can then determine whether the phrase was indeed copied and if more than just that particular phrase was used.

Even without these tools, an instructor can often detect work that does not belong to a particular student. Most instructors know the capabilities of their students and can usually figure out if a paper is written at a level above or below a student's usual standard. Students also write in their own style, so it may be obvious if suddenly one paper sounds different. Some parts of the paper may even be written in a different style than other parts, or some may use technical wording while others are written in everyday language. There have been some very obvious cases of plagiarism. Papers have been turned in with page numbers that are not sequential. Web addresses (URLs) have been left at the bottom of a printed page. Some papers have had different fonts at different points in the paper. While some of these are glaringly obvious cases of direct copying, instructors will be able to spot even the more subtle ones. Some instructors have educated themselves further about this problem. At the last minute, the instructor may ask you to hand in your rough notes along with your completed research paper. This will show beyond a doubt who has plagiarized information in a paper.

Using Abbreviations and Acronyms

It is helpful to use abbreviations and acronyms when you are taking notes. Not only does it speed up the process, it also takes up less space and is easier on your hands. This technique is especially useful when you are taking notes during an interview or when you are trying to take notes at a place such as a historical site, where you may not be able to spread out your books.

Many books can help you learn either shorthand or speedwriting. These will give you even further ideas to help you take notes quicker. Recommended titles include *Speedwriting for Notetaking and Study Skills* by Joe Pullis, *Gregg Shorthand* by Louis A. Leslie, *Quickhand* by Jeremy Grossman, and *EasyScript Express* by Leonard Levin.

Use the same abbreviations and acronyms throughout your project. You won't want to be trying to decipher what "bfr" means at the end of your project when you used "b4" in the first half of your notes. These are some common abbreviations that you can use:

ASAP—as soon as possible	gov't—government
Q—question	m/c—machine
A—answer	max—maximum
b/c—because	min—minimum
dept—department	prob—problem or probably
diff—difference	re—regarding
e.g.—for example	w/o—without
esp—especially	yr—year

You also can develop your own abbreviations if you are writing a particular word repeatedly. You may find it helpful to leave out any inconsequential words, such as "the," "an," and "for." You may just use a "g" for words that end in "ing." You should always use numerals (4) instead of writing out the word (four). You might also come up with your own acronyms. If your research paper deals with The Center for Sports Research and Injury Prevention, you may call it CSRIP in your notes, even though it may go by a completely different name in real life. However, CSRIP is much quicker and easier to write than is the full name.

ALERT!

You can get carried away with using acronyms and abbreviations. Don't use so many that your notes become illegible. Use the abbreviations that you can remember, but write out enough words so that you can make out the proper meaning. It shouldn't look like it was written in code.

Deciding What to Include

Some people have trouble deciding what is important enough to include in their notes and what is extraneous information, with the result that they leave out too much and end up with gaps in their information. Other times they take notes from everything they come across and end up with the big job of weeding out what isn't relevant. You should aim for somewhere in between these two extremes.

Facts

Factual information generally should be recorded. Usually this isn't a very time-consuming part of your note taking anyway. Later on in your research you may find uses for these facts, and at that point you won't want to go back and search for them again. If you're absolutely sure that the facts have no relationship to your topic, you can leave them out.

Don't be too quick to discard facts just because you think they are commonly known. For one thing, you could be more knowledgeable about your topic than is the average person, so what you think is a commonly known fact may not be. Also, sometimes these basic background facts are necessary supporting evidence for your research paper. Include them in your notes; you can always leave them out of the research paper if you find they are not needed later.

QUESTION?

What should I do if I find opposing information or viewpoints in different sources?
This is fine. Record both sides and be sure to list where each belief came from. A good research paper looks at all sides of the story and fully explores any contradictions.

Other Supporting Information

It is a little harder to ascertain the research value of some of the other supporting information you come across. Clearly, you should note the information directly related to your topic, and leave out the information that's definitely unrelated. But the majority of what you come across could lie in between. You will have to look closely at each piece of information to determine whether you need to make note of it or not. Does it add to the data you already have? Does it back up or substantiate your facts? Does it show a new and different view of things? Is it taking your research to a different level that you may or may not want to explore? These are some of the questions that could help you in deciding whether or not to include this information.

When in Doubt

Of course, there will be some information that you are undecided about. It will not always be clear if what you come across in your research will aid you in writing your research paper. The best thing to do when in doubt is to include it in your notes. You can always discard the information later on if you find it doesn't add anything to your research paper.

Staying Organized

You will gather a large quantity of notes during the research process. In order to make a smooth transition from notes to paragraphs, it is beneficial to organize those notes. The easiest time to start organizing them is right at the beginning. If you can develop a system for taking notes that ensures they are written down in an organized fashion, you will save yourself a lot of work later on.

Read First

It helps to read through written material before you start to take notes. Read a short section before you write down any notes. This means reading a paragraph or a page or however much it takes to get through one main idea. Doing this gives you a chance to digest the information and decide what parts of it are relevant. It also keeps you from taking too many notes, which would be unmanageable when you start to write your paper. In addition, you may also find it easier to write in your own words once you have the whole picture of that main idea.

Labeling Tips

Labeling each note is one way to keep them organized. As you take notes, jot down a heading that describes each note. Let's suppose you are writing a paper about downloading music. Your notes might be labeled under the headings of "music copyright laws" or "Napster history" or "typical download statistics." Always include the source of your information beside each note. This will make it a simple process to write your bibliography later on. Any notes that you decide to use as quotations should be clearly labeled as such, because you need to credit them. If you get in the habit of labeling each note you take, you will find it much easier to make an outline for your paper and to write the paper itself.

Headings or Separate Pages

You already know about choosing a method for writing your notes. If you use index cards, add a heading to each card. If you choose to use either regular paper or a computer, you need to take a different approach. You could use a separate page for the notes that come under each heading. This works as long as you have a good idea of what your headings will be right from the start. Otherwise you will end up having to rewrite notes from one page to another as you add new headings. If you work on a computer, you can create separate files for each note heading. Once the files are open, it is a simple matter to move around among them.

Add Your Own Thoughts

It is also an advantage to add any of your own thoughts and ideas to your notes. It is generally assumed that you will add this personal analysis later, when you write the draft versions of your paper. However, you may come up with some ideas at the time you take the notes. Instead of trying to remember these ideas later on, write them down with the note they refer to. Make sure you differentiate between the facts in the note and your own interpretation by using a different color pen or otherwise setting your ideas apart.

Allow Sufficient Space

One common note-taking mistake is not allowing enough room for the notes. Unless you work on a laptop, you will require a lot of index cards or a lot of paper, because you will record a lot of notes. Don't try to cram them into a small space. Leave yourself sufficient space for each note, its heading and source information, and your own thoughts. Record your notes on one side of the paper or index card only. This will make it much easier to organize your notes into a logical sequence later in the process.

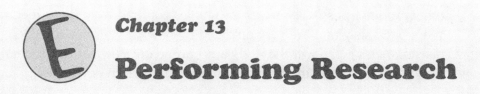

Chapter 13

Performing Research

So far, the focus of your work for your research paper has been on uncovering information that is already available. Now, you may find that it is time to perform your own research. You may need data that is more current than that already researched, or data that is more closely aligned with your particular topic. Your specific assignment may require you to do your own research.

Research Ideas

By this point you probably have a good idea about what your research project will be. There is often a gap in the type of information you are able to find from other sources. You may be unable to find a study related to your topic, or you may find many studies on that topic, but the results dispute each other. Another possibility is that the studies you find were performed many years previously and are very outdated by now, or you may discover some discrepancies in the way the study was carried out. Any of these scenarios is reason enough to augment your sources with research of your own.

Is Research Appropriate for You?

Whether or not you perform your own primary research is often dependent on the level you are at. If you are a high-school student, the scope of your project is likely to be much smaller, so extensive research of your own is probably not required. You may decide to do a short questionnaire or other simple research if you have the time or think it adds to the value of your research paper. You are unlikely to ever perform lab research at this level. On the other hand, you wouldn't work toward a Ph.D. without performing your own research. At this level your research will be very in-depth. You may perform experiments in a lab setting. You may undertake extensive questionnaires. You may lead focus groups through a series of discussions. At any level in between these two extremes, you may perform your own research to some degree.

No research work is entirely free of cost. At its most basic level, you may just incur photocopying expenses. A more involved, higher-level research project could involve a budget proposal and requests for funding, a topic you'll learn more about later in this chapter.

ALERT!

Your research will be much more valuable if it is unique. Research that uncovers something new interests everyone; research that simply confirms what is already known doesn't have much of a point to it. Try to design your study so that it will teach readers something original.

Generating a Hypothesis

You begin your research by writing a *hypothesis*. The hypothesis is a guess or prediction based on what you know so far about what you will find out from your research. This hypothesis will be similar to your thesis statement, but it needs to be in a form that is testable. It is usually the predicted answer to a question being asked or proven by your research.

Once you complete your research, you will discover whether your hypothesis is correct (valid) or incorrect (invalid). An invalid hypothesis does not mean that your research was bad. Nor does it mean that your hypothesis was a poor guess. It was based on what you knew at the time and what you supposed to be true. An invalid hypothesis only means that your research proved it to be wrong.

Using Previous Research as a Starting Point

You are quite likely to come across previous research projects that are related somehow to the project that you are about to do. You can use those projects as a starting point for your own. The key is to improve upon them or make any necessary changes so that they better suit your own project.

Refining a Study

One way to do this is to refine the previous study. There are a couple of different reasons why the previous study might not be appropriate for your needs. One reason could have to do with the lack of control over some of the variables in that study. A variable is a characteristic that the researcher strives to keep constant throughout the study and across all the participants in the study. These are the things that you would change and manipulate in order to gain results from your research. When a group of people are given higher doses of a drug to test their response to it, the dosage is a variable. When a puppy is introduced into a group of children to test their reactions, the puppy is a variable. When a group of cats are given different brands of food to see if they gain weight on a particular brand, the brands are variables. Variables can be present or absent; they can be used in different quantities; and the type of variable can change. Suppose the previous study you are interested in refining was done on the heart rates of children who grew up in homes with secondhand smoke. The variables that might not have been controlled were the amount of smoking in the home, the overall fitness level of each child, and the number of years the child was exposed to the secondhand smoke. You could do your own similar study, making sure that those variables were the same for all participants.

Make sure that you only change one variable in your study at a time. You will need to record what the variable was, how it changed, and by what amount it changed, if applicable. All other variables must remain constant. This is vital to ensure that you understand exactly what caused any change in results.

You might also want to conduct your research in a real-world setting. You could improve on a previous study by testing lab results in the actual setting in which they would be used. For instance, the earlier study you saw may have tested the physical response of a group of people who were chosen to give an impromptu speech in a lab. You might take that same concept into a classroom, call up students at random to give a speech, and test their physical responses there.

Duplicating a Study

Another way to make use of previous research is to try to duplicate a study. You need to follow the same procedures and use participants with the same characteristics. The object of this duplication is to verify the results. If your study does in fact duplicate the results, you will know that these are results in which you should have a great deal of confidence. You may come across two or more projects that attempted to prove the same hypothesis. However, if these studies came up with different results, you could perform your own research in this same area. Try to figure out why the previous studies varied. Were there variables that were not controlled? Was there something different in the methods that were used? Did they both follow the same procedure? Perform your research in the way you think best examines your hypothesis. This could be a blend of the procedures used in the previous studies. In some cases a previous research project will include suggestions for further study. Although that is sometimes stated clearly in the conclusion of the project, more often it is a subtle hint. Watch for references to aspects of the project that were not tested for, or variables that the researcher found difficult to control. The project may have ended when its purposes were fulfilled, but you may wish to carry it on further.

Objectives of Your Research

Obviously, the main objective of your research is to prove your hypothesis. In addition to this, there are five main research objectives, or types of results, that you can get from your research:

- Descriptive research—describes the traits and features of something.
- Explanatory research—shows the reasons why things occur the way they do.
- Exploratory research—offers new ideas about something.
- Influential or demonstrative research—applies results from the research to real situations and things.
- Predictive research—makes predictions. The level of accuracy is dependent on the topic of research.

Research Methods

The way you perform your research needs to be laid out in a precise fashion. Without a plan, your research will be haphazard and the results will be inconsistent. It is very important that you plan your research procedure carefully so that it will contribute toward the value of your entire project.

How to Collect Data

You can collect data in different ways. You need to choose which method suits your project based on the types of data you are seeking, the facilities you can use, how much money you have to spend on research, and the time you have available. In general, you collect data by using tests, questionnaires, interviews, focus groups, observation, and existing data.

Tests

Tests measure such things as achievement and personality qualities. They are a quick and easy way to get results, and those results end up being relatively easy to analyze. However, although most participants who write the test will respond to most of it, they may leave some questions unanswered. You need to have enough fully answered questions to gain a clear picture of the test results. Another downside to tests are the tests themselves. You can find standardized tests for purchase, but the cost may be prohibitive, leaving you to devise your own test. Even if you do decide to purchase a standardized test, you could have difficulty finding one that is appropriate for the group of respondents you want to target.

Questionnaires

Questionnaires are shorter, and therefore easier to create yourself. Because of this, they are inexpensive and can give quick, focused results. The participants know that their answers are completely anonymous, so they can give a more honest set of answers. On the other hand, because questionnaires are generally brief, some participants may not answer all of the questions or may misinterpret them. A questionnaire should do all of the following:

- stay relevant to the hypothesis
- use language that the participants will understand
- ask only one question at a time
- keep questions clear and brief
- avoid asking questions that lead the participant to a certain answer

If you are using a multiple-choice type of questionnaire, make sure that you list all possible answers. The participants should not have to choose from answers that don't really match their opinions. You could also consider changing the way you word each question, or changing the order of possible answers to avoid responses that are solely based on repetition. For instance, if all of the answers indicative of an outgoing personality are matched to the "A" option, the respondent will be tempted to always answer "A" without fully reading the question. Also, it is a good idea to get someone to test your questionnaire before you administer it. This should be someone with traits similar to those of your study participants.

Interviews

Interviews are one-on-one question-and-answer sessions that can be administered in person or over the phone. The advantage to using these rather than tests and questionnaires is that the interviewer can ask probing questions that result in in-depth information from the interviewee. There is a high response rate from interviews, and if any of the answers are incomplete, you can ask them again. Of course, there is always a downside to any research method. Interviews do take much longer to administer than do many other research methods. The extra time may be worth it, however, because interviewees frequently speak impulsively and candidly. Some of the answers may not be well thought out, but at the same time they can be revealing. The quality of these answers will vary with the level of comfort the interviewee has with you, and may differ depending on personality, because in-person interviews do not allow for anonymity.

Focus Groups

Focus groups optimally are made up of six to twelve people who answer questions and discuss a particular topic. They are joined by a moderator, whose job it is not only to ask the questions but also to keep the group from straying off topic. You can plan on a focus group discussion lasting up to three hours. It is most informative to either videotape or audiotape the session. With so many people to keep track of, it can be hard to remember who said what. Also, you can determine nuances afterward by watching a video or listening to a tape. Focus groups can provide in-depth information, and they are a quick way to get responses from several people. It would take much longer to interview each one of them separately.

The way that the participants react to one another can have a positive or negative effect on the outcome of the focus group. The participants may encourage each other to open up about issues, or to bring forth an opposing view. The opposite may also occur. Some participants may not feel comfortable with the others, and therefore may not share their true feelings. One or two more vocal participants can dominate the entire discussion. And if the moderator doesn't keep the discussion focused, you may end up with unnecessary information.

Observation

When you use observation as a research method, you watch what the participants do. There are a number of different ways you can do this. You can observe them in a lab setting or in a natural setting, which could be students in a classroom, animals in a field, or children at a playground, for instance. They might know you are observing them, or you might be an anonymous observer. If the participants know that you are observing them, they might not act as naturally as you would like, but they could also cooperate more easily if you want to give them some direction or have some control over what they do. The observation method enables you to see what participants do, not what they say they do, or what others say they do. You can also see what they do not do. This can be a helpful research method if participants don't have good verbal skills, as is the case with young children or people without strong English skills. Observation also is a good research method when animals are the participants. However, some settings may be difficult for observation. If you are observing children at a playground, you might look suspicious. If you try to bring those same children into a lab setting, you incur a high cost.

QUESTION?

What if I can't decide which research method to use?
Your research will actually be more accurate if you use more than one method. However, if you don't have the time or the budget to do that, try to determine the optimal method by considering which one will give you the most accurate results.

Existing Data

Finally, you may decide to use existing data. This could be data from a similar study. You could use data that was discovered in a previous research project and interpret and analyze it your own way. The previous project may not even be related to your own. The data could be a byproduct of research that was done to prove a different hypothesis, but is still useful to you.

Sampling Types

No matter what method of research you choose, you need to find participants. These are referred to as your *samples*, because they are a sample representation of an overall population. All samples should be as large as you can handle in order to give more reliable results. There are different methods of sampling that you can use, depending on whether you are looking for quantitative results (those with a numerical value) or qualitative results (those that are verbal or visual). If you were looking for quantitative results, you could use the following:

- Simple random samples—selected completely at random.
- Systematic random samples—selecting every nth participant from a list.
- Stratified random samples—selecting a certain number of participants from each base group (for example, selecting from those living in apartments, houses, and mobile homes).
- Convenience nonrandom samples—selecting the participants who are most easily available.
- Quota nonrandom samples—selecting a certain number of participants from each of certain groups (for example, selecting five participants from each age group that you set).
- Purposive nonrandom samples—selecting participants who display specific characteristics (for example, selecting men aged twenty-five or older who live with their parents).
- Snowball nonrandom samples—selecting a few participants with a specific characteristic and getting them to refer others to you with that same characteristic. This is useful when the respondents you seek are difficult to identify (for example, those with a rare disease).

If you were looking for qualitative results, you could use these:

- Maximum variation sampling—selecting a wide range of participants.
- Homogeneous sampling—selecting a small group of participants and studying them intensively.

- Extreme case sampling—selecting participants from the extreme ends of the spectrum being studied.
- Typical case sampling—selecting participants who are average in terms of the research topic.
- Critical case sampling—selecting the most important cases.
- Negative case sampling—selecting participants who oppose your theories or who refute your theories.
- Opportunistic sampling—selecting useful participants whenever opportunity presents them.
- Mixed purposeful sampling—selecting participants by using a mixture of these methods.

Consent of Participants

Any participants in your research must give their consent to take part. This consent should be in written form, and they should know that they can withdraw from participation at any time. If you are using juvenile participants, you need to get their parents or guardians to sign a consent form for them. The consent form should include a brief statement of the purpose of the research. It should also include a summary of the procedures that will be followed, the length of time required for participation, a description of any risks or discomforts the participant may experience, a statement of confidentiality, and the amount they will be paid for participation, if that applies.

Collaborating with Others

You may have thought of your research paper as being your own personal project, but there are benefits to collaborating with someone else when you perform your own research. You can collaborate on this segment of your paper and then do the rest of it on your own.

You may not be aware of the benefits of researching with someone else. Performing research is an intense, time-consuming process. No matter which method of research you decide to use, it is helpful to have someone working with you. You can always use more than one viewpoint when it comes to designing the research, asking questions, and interpreting the results. If you are working with someone on your project, you are more likely to receive higher amounts of funding, and your paper may be more likely to eventually be published.

If this is your first research project, you could benefit from working with a mentor. Many universities have mentoring programs whereby faculty members or people from the professional community work alongside a student on their research. This teaches the student many things. It helps the student understand how to run research procedures without making costly mistakes. It gives the student access to labs and equipment that he or she otherwise may not be able to use. It teaches the student to follow proper safety procedures. A peer review also can be helpful. This allows the student to gain feedback from others who are not closely involved with the research project and may be able to clearly see things that the researcher missed.

Project Funding

All of this research has a cost associated with it. You need to know what costs you will incur in order to carry out the research the way you plan. Then you need to decide how to pay for it.

FACT

There are many opportunities for grants, from a wide variety of sources. There is also a lot of competition for that grant money, so your application needs to stand out above the rest. Make sure you follow all the rules for each particular grant. Include all the requested details, and get your application in by the deadline.

What Costs Are Involved?

The costs you will incur vary greatly depending on the research method or methods you use, the number of participants, and the topic you are researching. You can plan to have certain items included in your costs, including any extra staffing you require to carry out your research. For instance, if you have someone help you videotape your focus group, you might want to pay the videographer for her or his time. If you require the use of a lab for your research, you need to pay for it. You may also need to make some long-distance phone calls for your research. Travel costs, including gas or any other trip-related expenses, must be figured into your costs as well. There also are costs for special equipment you use and for any consumables, such as postage, photocopying, or audiocassettes.

Applying for Grants

Luckily, there is grant money available to fund research projects. This money comes from government agencies and from private or corporate sponsorship. Your instructor should be able to tell you what is available in your area and at your level. You need to apply for these grants, submitting a research proposal when you apply. Though the funding can depend on external factors, such as a particular organization's grant cycle or topic range, a well-written proposal helps greatly in your chances for acceptance. A research proposal should include a statement of the topic, a discussion of previous relevant research, and the hypothesis. It should disclose the specific procedure that you will follow and identify any equipment or instruments that you will use. It should also specify the number of participants who will be used, and the criteria for their selection. In addition, you should describe how you plan to analyze the data that results from your research.

Collating Research Results

Once you complete your research, you will be left with the data it produced. What you do with that data is just as important as how you gathered it. You need to look again at your hypothesis to see how the data relates to it.

Your research needs to go one step further than simply collecting raw data. You need to determine how the variables you used affected the outcomes of your study and how these results can be transferred to a real-life application. The relationships you uncover should all relate back to your purpose.

Questions to Ask

You will have extensive notes and data gathered during your research, but you may not be certain how to combine these into a cohesive paper. You can ask a number of questions in order to figure out how to best use and present your data.

- Could the results from your sample group be projected to a larger group?
- Could the results from your experiment or research be projected to a different place?
- Could the results be projected to a different time period?
- When certain variables change, how does the outcome of the research change?
- Is there some way to categorize the results?

If you have a large amount of data, you may want to use a database program to sort it, or you could use special data analysis software. This includes such programs as these:

- AnSWR—*www.cdc.gov/hiv/software/answr.htm*
- HyperRESEARCH—*www.researchware.com/hr/index.html*
- N6—*www.qsr.com.au/products/productoverview/product_overview.htm*
- Transana—*www.transana.org*

Common Errors

Any research contains some degree of error. This is important to remember not only for your own research, but when you read the results from the research of others as well. Because each research method has its own strengths and weaknesses, it is best to use multiple research methods whenever possible. There are many reasons why errors can occur. When different people take measurements or record observations, they may use different methods or interpret the data differently. When you are collaborating with a partner, you should make sure that you either both record these things in the same way or that the same person does it always.

You should be careful not to let your own biases cloud your judgment. Record what you see, not what you want to see or what you had expected to see. Sometimes you might not be able to differentiate between the cause of an occurrence and the effect of that occurrence, and this can result in errors. The participants themselves may cause the errors in the study. They may perceive the answers you want to find and adjust their responses accordingly on an unconscious level. They may decide not to continue on with a study they have started in, or they may answer some questions but not others. There could also be external factors that cause errors. If your participants are young, their responses could change over time as they grow up, and a long term study could reflect those changes. In as short a time frame as a few months, their responses may have changed.

Some variables may be difficult to control if the research takes place over a period of time. You can try to control the reliability of your research results by employing a few different techniques. You can test the same group of participants a number of different times to see if their responses are the same. You can administer similar tests to the same group of people. You would design these tests to measure the same thing in a different manner. Ideally, you would end up with similar results no matter how the test is administered. You can also measure reliability by having more than one person observe and record results. This should keep the personal biases of the researcher from affecting what is recorded.

Chapter 14

Assessing and Analyzing Information

Gathering research is much more than a process of simply regurgitating the data and information you find. You must be able to figure out what is truly relevant to your topic and what is worthy of inclusion in your paper. You are likely to discard some of the research you carry out and find other things that are enlightening. You must be able to interpret what you find and draw out what you need in order to pursue your thesis.

Types of Data

You will discover different types of data in your research. You probably will combine all of these types to form the background of your paper. When you understand the differences among these types, you can determine which type of data you are looking at and how it should be used in your research.

ALERT!

Factual data is often collected through three different methods. These are a census, a sample survey, or administrative data. A census collects data from every person or thing in a group. A sample survey collects data from a smaller part of that group. Administrative data is that which is collected as part of an organization's ongoing function.

Factual Data and Information

Factual data is the type of data that deals with hard statistics. Any data that deals with numbers is likely to be factual data, including populations, percentages, sizes, statistics, and distances. Factual data isn't typically open to interpretation, although it can be used to identify trends.

QUESTION?

Should I still use data that I think is biased?
Yes, but with caution. You can never use the data while ignoring the fact that it is biased. You need to take the bias into account in your analysis. How you do that will depend largely on the type of data it is and the topic of your paper.

Biased Data and Information

When data or information is dependent on someone's opinions, that data becomes biased. This is generally not the case so much with specific facts, but with more general information. If you interviewed an expert on rehabilitating habitual criminals and that person stated that no habitual criminal he or she had ever dealt with was ever completely "cured," that would be biased data. It is based on that person's perceptions of the situation. Data can also be biased even when it appears to be factual. For example, if a survey of test scores were taken of students at a local college, you would need to make sure that the survey included either all students or a broad cross section of students. The results would be skewed if the survey only included the top students or the male students or the students with part-time jobs. Of course, if you are looking only for that subset of results that is fine, but you need to be clear about what results you are looking at.

Biased data isn't completely useless. It can reflect the thoughts and feelings of particular people or of a society in general. It can show how certain situations affect certain outcomes, as in the example of the student test scores. In order for the data to be useful, you need to know that it is biased and how it is biased. You also may be personally biased in a particular direction. You might interpret what you read or see or hear to mean something different than what it does because of your preconceived ideas. These could be ideas about the topic or about the source of the information itself. Be careful to compare what you read and see and hear with what is available elsewhere to determine whether you are allowing your own bias to get in the way of your research.

Inferential data is used to make predictions or estimations. You can assume that if a certain segment of a population does things one way, that same percentage of a larger population will also do things that way. It is not a hard fact, however, so inferential data should be used with caution in your research paper.

Inferential Data and Information

Inferential data can be difficult to identify. It may appear to be highly factual when instead the facts were used to make an estimate about the data. What was found in the facts is used to make a generalization or to infer something about a larger group. For instance, if the facts state that 50 percent of the residents of a small town are Catholic, one might infer that

50 percent of the residents of that town attend the Catholic church in their town. That statement makes a lot of assumptions. Despite the fact that some of the residents claim to be Catholic, they might not attend church at all. Those who do attend church might attend a different church in that town or a Catholic church in a different town or a different church in a different town. The problem lies in the fact that if you had found the statement that claimed that 50 percent of the residents of that town attended the Catholic church in their town, you might assume that it was factual data. Be careful to look at the source of all of your data in order to clarify its accuracy.

Types of Sources

A well-rounded paper includes information from many different types of sources. However, some instructors set guidelines regarding the types of sources you can use for your research paper. The two main types of sources are primary sources and secondary sources. If your instructor issues guidelines restricting the number or type of sources you may use, you need to be able to distinguish between them.

Primary Sources

A primary source is the original appearance of information or data. It has not been edited or evaluated in any manner. Primary sources often relay new information and are commonly printed at the time an event occurred, or soon afterward. Further research is based on primary sources, but primary sources are not based on any other research. These are some examples of primary sources:

- Statistical data
- Photos
- Autobiographies
- Speeches
- Interviews
- Minutes from a meeting
- Legal documents

If you have difficulty finding primary source material, you can make use of some of the information included in the secondary source material. For instance, an encyclopedia entry about a specific event might mention people and groups that were closely involved in the event. You could then look for primary source material that came directly from those people or groups. You could look for their publications, such as a brochure put out by group, or diaries and letters written by the people involved.

Secondary Sources

Once information from a primary source is evaluated, analyzed, or otherwise modified, it is a secondary source. These sources provide some comment on the original data and are therefore one step further removed from the source. Sometimes it can be difficult to determine whether a source is primary or secondary. For instance, a newspaper can be either one depending on whether it is reporting facts (primary) or providing commentary on those facts (secondary). Some examples of secondary sources are:

- Biographies
- Some magazine and newspaper articles
- Some textbooks
- Some encyclopedias
- Review articles
- Bibliographies

Secondary source documents include an analysis, similar to what you do with your information as your write your research paper. This analysis could be persuasive in nature, or it could hold a certain opinion about an issue, but this is not always the case. Some secondary source information is fairly objective, such as that in an encyclopedia entry.

Tertiary Sources

Tertiary sources are closely related to secondary sources. Sources are considered tertiary when they combine information from primary and secondary sources. These are sometimes a repackaging of the material contained in a secondary source. Some examples of tertiary sources are:

- Almanacs
- Guidebooks
- Chronologies
- Some dictionaries
- Some textbooks
- Some encyclopedias

You often can use tertiary sources to help you find primary and secondary sources. This can be helpful early in the research process if you aren't sure where to look for the information you want.

Indicators of Reliability

The sources of information you find may include a wide range of accuracy, value, and suitability. Some sources are extremely valuable and well focused for your topic. Others are not as reliable or well rounded. Still others are just not a good fit with your type of research. You can check a few different aspects of your source to ensure that it is good for your purposes. What constitutes a good source for one paper is not necessarily a good source for another paper. The following sections show you what to look for as you evaluate the materials you find.

Documentation

You should be able to see where the research source got its information. Statistical data in particular should be documented so that you know exactly where the data came from. If there is no bibliographical information shown for your source, there should be some contact information for the author. Just because someone makes some claims doesn't mean you should automatically trust those claims to be true. Be especially wary if the source makes claims that are different from those you have seen or heard elsewhere. In such a case, be sure that the author included facts and background documentation as the source of those claims. If you question the credibility of a fact, try to verify it against another reliable source so that you are assured it is a fact and not just an interpretation.

Authority of Sources

Be sure that the author or the source itself is known to be reliable. Some publications, such as encyclopedias, almanacs, journals, and textbooks, are well respected and known to only publish accurate information. When the source is less recognized, you need to check for the author's credentials. Find out whether the author has specific experience or education that qualifies her or him to write about the subject. What is the author's job title? Sometimes an author's contact information is provided, so you can ask for more details if needed. If other respected sources cite this author, you can be fairly confident that the source in question is a reliable one.

The purpose of the source can affect the reliability of the information. If the source exists to persuade or influence the reader or viewer in any way, the information it contains may be distorted somewhat. For example, a company that sells lawn products may distribute a "fact sheet" or short video about garden pests. These materials, however, will recommend the company's products as the solution; they will not recommend alternative methods for dealing with unwanted bugs.

Suitability of Sources

Even when a source is found to be reliable, it may not be suitable for your paper. The intended audience of the source could be much less experienced or much more experienced than you are. That will determine whether the information is too general or too specific and technical for your paper. The information may have been written for a very different purpose than yours, and therefore has a completely different slant on things. Be particularly careful if your source is a Web site. The purpose of the Web site will in many cases help determine its reliability and suitability for research. Web sites can be categorized into a few different types:

- Organizational Web sites
- Government Web sites

- Academic Web sites
- Commercial Web sites
- Personal Web sites
- Interest Group and Association Web sites

You can see that some of these types of sites are more likely to be reliable sources. Some sites exist for reasons other than simply providing information. They may be selling something, trying to convince you of their position, or even attacking other groups. In addition, not all the Web sites of one type will be equally reliable. It may take some detective work on your part to uncover the reliability of a source, including those you are inclined to trust automatically.

Timely Sources

You should look at the publication date of the source you are using. If you are writing about a historical topic, the primary sources should have been published close to the time of the event. Secondary sources published after the event will be reliable if the research was reputable. If your project deals with a more current event, timeliness is even more important. Be sure that major changes haven't occurred between the publication of your source and the time you are using the source. It can be hard to know how timely Web site information is, because sometimes no date is shown on the site. Even when a date is shown, it is not always clear whether that is the date when the information was first put there or when it was last revised.

Quantity and Diversity of Sources

It is easier to trust a source when you have seen the same information come from another source. Therefore, a quantity of sources is a good thing to have. On the other hand, you need sources that are diverse. A variety of different sources offering a variety of information and interpretations gives you enough resource material to fully explore and explain all aspects of your topic. These aspects can include many different viewpoints, and even opposing viewpoints.

Types of Data

There are two basic types of data you will come across in your research: quantitative and qualitative. It is fairly simple to differentiate between these two types, and once you can you will understand how to use each type. To ensure that your research is robust, you should use both types of data whenever possible.

Quantitative Data

Quantitative, or numeric, data refers to data that measures something. This type of data consists of numbers instead of words. It is more often thought of as hard, scientific data that is easier to report, but harder to interpret. Most often it backs up qualitative data, but occasionally you might find that it contradicts such data. That is where some interpretation is required.

Some of the results of your research could be quantitative, producing numerical data that measures something related to your topic. For example, your research may involve collecting data on the number of traffic accidents involving drivers of various age groups. As part of your project, you not only present the data, you interpret it. Your job is to uncover the reasons why certain drivers are involved in more, or fewer, accidents.

FACT

You can gather quantitative data much more quickly than you can qualitative data. You can survey a large amount of responses for quantitative data, and then easily sort and analyze the responses by using computer software programs. Gathering qualitative data is a much slower process, and it's followed by an analysis that is sometimes impossible to automate.

Qualitative Data

Qualitative data refers to data represented by words, text, photos, sound recordings, films, and basically anything else that is not numeric. This type of data may be more open to interpretation, depending on the topic. It requires more description to report, because it is less factual. You can gather qualitative data in several different ways. You could use historical research that involves interviewing witnesses or analyzing documents, photos, and other artifacts from the time in question. You could use case studies, in which you interview or observe the people or person that the research is about. You could use personal interviews or focus groups, in which the people involved have the opportunity to answer direct questions. You also can use questionnaires, which give people the chance to add their thoughts about a specific issue.

Analyzing Research

When you reach the point at which you are ready to analyze your findings, you will ask many questions. This is the main point of your research paper. You want to determine the validity of the information you found and how it relates to your paper. Although you are likely to have a significant amount of information to analyze, remembering a few main points will help keep you focused.

Don't twist the data through your analysis in order to suit the purpose of your research paper. It is sometimes tempting to see what you want to see in the data you collect instead of seeing what is really there. You need to be objective in your analysis.

You know what your thesis is, and you have kept that in mind as a goal while you gathered research. It is just as important now to focus on that purpose of your paper. Your purpose should dictate how you analyze your research, rather than the other way around. You should always ask how the information you found through your research relates back to the overall purpose of your research paper. If your paper poses a question that you want to answer, you should have information that supports your answer. You need to show how you arrived at your conclusions, not just provide background information and jump to the conclusion.

It's possible that your research revealed some unexpected or contradictory results. Though this adds a certain challenge, it makes your work that much more interesting. Suppose your research paper were about the sleep patterns of older people. You expected older people to be much lighter sleepers, and you assumed that they would need less sleep overall but would space it out more evenly over a twenty-four-hour period. You conducted some surveys and convinced some senior citizens to track their sleep habits for a few weeks. For the most part, their responses were just as you had expected. However, a group of three women reported vastly different sleep habits. They were deep sleepers who still got a full nine hours of sleep consistently every night and never slept during the day. Because of these contradictory results, you need to do some further analysis of your data. In this case, you might ask the participants to also track their activities during their waking hours. What you eventually find out is that these three women are friends who get together every day to hike five miles. Their strenuous exercise regime keeps them from developing the sleep habits of others their age.

When you do get unexpected or contradictory results, you need to look into them further. It isn't enough to just report results; find out why you got the results you did. Be able to explain any unusual data, so that it does not appear to be the result of a flaw in your research methods.

Chapter 15

Writing a Bibliography

A bibliography is a record of all the sources you use in compiling your paper. It is always included in every type of project that involves any research. This key section shows that you used accurate and well-rounded sources of information, and credits those sources. There are a few different formats that are commonly used, including the MLA (Modern Language Association) and the APA (American Psychological Association).

Start Early!

Perhaps the biggest mistake you can make with your bibliography is to leave it until you finish writing the paper. This is a very common error, and it results in a lot more work than if you started it early. By the time you finish writing the paper, you have returned books and other borrowed material; reference materials you used on-site have been reshelved; and you may have even forgotten about some sources you used. Too often students don't think about the bibliography until the end because it is usually the last page of the project. It is even listed last under the requirements for the project. However, it should be started at the same time that the research work begins.

FACT

Some instructors refer to a bibliography by another name, such as references, works cited, list of sources, or research credits. Whatever name they use, it is the same thing. If you are not told what to call it, you should refer to it as the bibliography.

Add as You Go

There are two schools of thought about what to include in a bibliography. Some people believe that only the sources for the notes you actually use to write the body of your paper should appear in the bibliography. If that's the method that you choose, you might want to record each note's source beside that note as you take it. Then, when you use a particular note, you can add easily add its source to the bibliography. The second method is to record every source you use for your notes directly into the bibliography. The rationale for this is that once you have read or heard or watched a particular source, it is subconsciously recorded in your mind, whether you use that specific note in your paper or not. The ideas from that source still inform your thoughts and opinions on the topic. Of course, if you use a direct quote, you need to cite the source with the quote and also include the information in the bibliography.

Whichever method you choose, it is advantageous to record your sources as you work through the research portion of your project. Every time you use a new source, you should note it in your bibliography. You should still record page numbers in your notes, because you may need to recheck information later. If you keep adding to the bibliography as you go, it will be complete when you are finished researching your topic.

FACT

Several popular guides describe how to write a bibliography. The most common is the MLA. Another frequently used style is the APA. Other style guides you may also come across include the Chicago/Turabian, the Harvard, the *Columbia Guide to Online Style* (CGOS), and the CBE (Council of Biology Editors).

Retain Material

Whenever possible, retain your research material until you finish the project. This means not returning books to the library until your work is done, and printing hard copies of material you find on the Internet. If you must return library books, it's a good idea to photocopy the copyright page for future reference. You should also keep contact information for anyone you interviewed. Of course, many of the resources you use for a research paper cannot be taken home. Microfilm and microfiche, historical documents, and photos are prime examples of resources that can only be used in their respective libraries, museums, or archives. Make photocopies or printouts whenever possible, and keep those and their source notations until your work is done.

QUESTION?

Why is a bibliography necessary?
A bibliography provides proof of your research. It shows that the facts you include are documented elsewhere, that the thoughts you present as being those of others actually were written or spoken, and that the things you viewed are in existing photos. It also provides more information should someone want to look into your topic further.

Citing Books and Other Printed Material

You are likely to use books, magazines, journals, newspapers, and encyclopedias in your research. While the formats for citing these sources are similar, there are some things that are peculiar to each particular type of resource. Make sure that every citation has the information in the correct order. Different guides may order or style the parts of a citation a bit differently; make sure that the style you choose is applied consistently throughout the bibliography. There are no headings in a bibliography letting you know, for instance, what is a title and what is a publisher, so you must always follow a standard style.

Format for Books

Books are listed alphabetically in a bibliography according to the author's last name, and then the first name. The exact title of the book, including a subtitle if there is one, is the next element of the entry. Depending on the style guide you are following, this title will either be underlined or italicized. MLA style calls for underlined titles, and APA style calls for italics, so check with your instructor to find out whether he or she has a preference. You need to record the city in which the book was published, the name of the publisher, and the year of publication of the latest edition. If it is a subsequent edition, note which one it is. Most of this information should be found on one of the first pages in the book.

A typical book citation looks like this (note the italicized title and the periods, commas, and colons):

Hammer, Willie. *Occupational Safety Management and Engineering*. 3rd edition. Englewood Cliffs, N.J.: Prentice-Hall, Inc., 1985.

Once you decide on a format, be sure to use it consistently throughout your paper.

If there a two authors for a book, the first author's name is listed with the last name first. The second author's name is listed with the first name first.

Here is an example of a citation for a book by two authors:

Nist, Sherrie and Jodi Patrick Holschuh. *College Rules! How to Study, Survive, and Succeed in College*. Berkeley, CA: Ten Speed Press, 2002.

When a book has more than two authors, only the first one is noted, followed by "et al." This is a Latin term meaning "and others."

Here is an example of a citation for a book by more than two authors:

Leenders, Michiel R. et al. *Purchasing and Materials Management.* 8th edition. Homewood, IL: Richard D. Irwin, Inc., 1985.

ALERT!

Make sure you understand the difference between a regular bibliography and an annotated bibliography. A regular bibliography is what's described in this chapter. An annotated bibliography includes a brief description after each citation that tells what a writer thinks is the value and relevance of each source. You are not likely to ever include an annotated bibliography in a research paper.

Format for Magazines and Journals

The citation for magazines and journals follows the same format whether they are mainstream publications or those of a technical nature. Again, they are listed alphabetically by the author's last name. The titles of both the article and the publication are noted, as is the date of publication. This citation also notes the pages on which the particular article is found.

Here is an example of a citation for a magazine or journal article. Note that the title of the article is in quotation marks and that only the first word of the title is capitalized:

Struzik, Ed. "Grizzlies on ice." *Canadian Geographic* November/December 2003: 38–48.

Format for Newspapers

Newspaper article citations are very similar to those of magazines and journals. The entry begins with the author's name and the title of the article. This is followed by the title of the newspaper and the day, month, year, and edition in which the article was printed. You also must include the page number or numbers.

This is an example of a citation for a newspaper article:

Maharaj, Davan. "The $10 impossible dream: A year of school" *Los Angeles Times* 20 July 2004: C2.

Again, check the style guide you are using to determine whether the name of the newspaper should be underlined or italicized. Some guides also place the date before the name of the newspaper.

Format for Encyclopedias

Citations for encyclopedias are unique in that you show the number of total volumes along with the number of the volume that you used as your source. You also include the writer's and the editor's names if they are given, the title of the article, the title of the encyclopedia, the edition, the place and year of publication, and the pages on which the article was found.

Here is a sample citation for an encyclopedia article (the numbers at the end of the citation are the volume number, then a colon, followed by the page number):

"Julius Caesar." *The Golden Home and High School Encyclopedia*. 1st edition. 20 vols. New York, NY: Golden Press, 1961. 10:1366.

ALERT!

The Internet is a very quickly developing and changing medium. As it evolves, guidelines for new features are likely to be missing in any but the most current style guide. Use your best judgment to cite these new sources. It is better to collect more information than to leave out something vital. Again, strive for consistency.

Citing the Internet

While the Internet has created an added realm of opportunity for research, it has also added a challenge for bibliographies. Information posted on the Internet can come and go quickly, or it can move to another location. There is currently no standard for some of the contact information posted online, so it may be more difficult to cite some sources than it is others.

Format for Web Sites

A Web site citation includes the editor's name, the title of the article, the date it was written, the name of the site or organization, the date you accessed the site, and the URL (address).

This is an example of a Web site citation:

Isaacs, Kim. "Ten Classic Resume Bloopers: Know Them So You Won't Make Them." Monster Resume Center 18 Oct 2004. <http://resume.monster. com/articles/bloopers/>

Format for Newsgroups

The citation for a newsgroup discussion includes the writer's name, the subject line, the phrase "online posting," the date of the post, the date of access, and the name of the newsgroup.

Here is an example of a newsgroup discussion:

Greg G. "Graphic Designers—Coping with Computer Upgrades." Online posting. 30 Mar 2004. 27 Sept 2004. <comp.graphics.animation>

Format for E-mail Messages

A citation for an e-mail message includes the sender's name, the subject line, a description of the message, and the date it was sent.

This is an example of an e-mail message citation:

Jones, Mary. "Update on project." E-mail to George Wingood. 12 Aug 2003.

Format for Forums or Message Board Discussions

Information you glean from a forum or message board discussion also must be cited. The correct format for this includes the writer's name, the title of the posting, the phrase "online posting," the date of the post, the name of the forum, the date you accessed it, and the URL.

Here is an example of a forum discussion citation:

Barbe2. "Tutoring Services." Online posting. 16 Oct 1999. Homework/Study Tips Forum. 9 Jan 2002 http://forums.about.com/ab-homeworkhelp/ messages?lgnF=y&msg=43.1

Format for Listserver or Mailing List Discussions

Citations for listserver or mailing list discussions include the writer's name, the subject line, the phrase "online posting," the date of posting, the name of the listserver, the date of access, and the address of the listserver.

This is an example of a citation for a listserver discussion:

Smythe, Bob. "Re: Cost saving ideas." Online posting. 30 June 1995. Europe Travel. 5 July 1995 <list@europetravel.com>

Citing Films and Television

Research that you conduct in a visual or auditory form also must be included in your bibliography. Such research falls under two categories. One category is films, videos, and movies that are produced for personal viewing, while the other is television and radio that are produced for broadcast.

Format for Films and Videos

Citations for films and videos should include the title, series title, director or producer, main actors, release or version, format you watched, name of the studio or distributor, and the original release date. Not all of these details will always be available. Here is a sample citation for a movie:

Cat Ballou. Dir. Elliot Silverstein. Perfs. Jane Fonda, Lee Marvin, Michael Callan. Video. Columbia Pictures, 1965.

Format for Television and Radio

Citations for media that is broadcast include the program title, series, writer, producer, director, performers, the network, call letters of the local affiliate you heard or watched it on, the city that affiliate is in, and the date of the broadcast.

A television or radio citation should look something like this:

"A Daring Rescue from an Arizona Religious Sect." Prod. *Primetime Live*. ABC. WRTV, Indianapolis. 4 Mar 2004.

When you record a citation for broadcast media, some of the details are more important than others for certain shows. Performers could be more important in a reenactment of an event while producers and directors could be more important in a scenic film. For example, when listing the writer, producer, director, and performers, list the most important ones first, and work toward the least important or visible. (Some of these job titles are simply not applicable to a particular program.)

Citing Information from Museums

Much of the information you find in museums is similar to that found elsewhere. You may use films, books, or newspapers from museums, which you will list in your bibliography in the same manner as similar resources found elsewhere. Some materials, however, are unique to the museum.

Many of the citations you include in your bibliography will not contain all of the information that is described here. Include as much of this information as you can find, and be sure you are looking in the right place. If you find that some of the details are missing, you should ask someone knowledgeable before leaving those details out.

Format for Written Information from Museums

You may find information in letters or other written materials at a museum. When citing these you include the name of the writer, the name of the recipient, the date the material was written, a name given to the collection if applicable, and the name and location of the museum.

This is an example of a citation for written material:

Jackson, Sheldon. Letter to Otis Tufton Mason. 31 Dec 1895. National Anthropological Archives, Smithsonian Institution Museum Support Center, Suitland, MD.

Format for Photographic Information from Museums

If you use information found in a photo, you need to include that photo as a source in your bibliography. The citation should include the photographer's name, the title of the photo, the date it was taken, the date you viewed it, and the name of the place where you viewed it. If applicable, you should also include a Web site address and digital ID where the photo can be viewed.

Here is an example of a citation for a photo:

Webster & Stevens. "Sailing for Alaska." 1905 or 1906. 20 Oct 2004. Seattle's Museum of History & Industry.

Information that you received firsthand from a source should be included whether or nor there was a formal interview. If you asked someone a question, whether verbally or by mail or e-mail, and the response is included in your research paper, that person is a source and the response must be be cited.

Citing Interviewees

Information you received directly from other people also must be cited in your bibliography. These personal communications are still sources, even if they are verbal, handwritten, or electronic sources.

Make sure that the sources for any quotes in the body of your research paper are included in your bibliography. You must note your source in your paper immediately following the quote (you are doing that, right?), but this does not take the place of a citation in the bibliography. These rules apply whether the quote came from a personal interview or from a source recorded elsewhere.

Format for Personal Interviews

You do need to briefly cite personal interviews. The citation should include the name of the interviewee, whether the interview was conducted in person or by telephone, via e-mail or "snail" mail, and the date of the interview.

This is an example of a personal interview citation:

Blakely, Kris. Telephone interview. 21 Jan 1999.

Format for Questionnaires

If you choose to use questionnaires as a research source, you also need to cite these in your bibliography. What you actually cite is the collection of questionnaires as a whole, not each one separately. Include the name of the surveyor (which will be your own name in this case), the title of the questionnaire, and the date it was administered.

Here is an example of a citation for questionnaires:

Sanderson, Viv. "Do You Live a Healthy Lifestyle?" 16 May 2001.

Putting It All Together

After you finish gathering all your citations, you need to put them together into one bibliography. There is a specific way to do this, but it is fairly straightforward.

You must present all of your citations in alphabetical order. List them all together no matter what form they took. Books, videos, interviews, and any other sources are all part of the same list; do not break them up into different segments. You determine the alphabetical order by the first item that is listed in each citation, as shown in this chapter. In most cases this is the last name of an author or a photographer, but in some cases it is the title of a television show or a video. When an item begins with "the," "a," or "an," disregard this word for alphabetizing purposes.

Your instructor will tell you what heading to use on your citation page. It is usually "Works Cited" or "Bibliography." This heading is centered on the page, but not underlined. Each citation is listed in order after that with no extra spacing. Each citation begins at the left of the page. If it continues on to two or more lines, all consecutive lines are indented. The next citation begins again at the left of the page.

Does it really matter if I use commas or colons in specific places?
Bibliographies do contain a lot of details in punctuation. You should know, though, that these are rules, not just suggestions, and you need to follow them exactly. It is important to follow the style rules consistently.

Footnotes and Endnotes

Check with your syllabus to see whether footnotes and endnotes are required. Some instructors want to see them on all research papers, while others have completely done away with them. If they are required, there is a specific format to use. The following sections explain how these notes are used, and how you should format them.

Footnotes and endnotes are another way to credit the source of the material used for research. They are used in addition to a bibliography. Instead of simply listing the sources as a bibliography does, these notes take readers to the exact page on which the material was found. Footnotes and endnotes are also used to present additional information that may not fit directly into the section to which it is related.

How Footnotes and Endnotes Differ

Though footnotes and endnotes are shown in the text of the paper in the same way, the listing of the sources is done differently. You will use either footnotes or endnotes, but not both. Footnotes are listed at the bottom (or foot) of the page on which the source is referenced. Endnotes are listed on a separate page at the end of the research paper, just before the bibliography. This page is called "Endnotes" or sometimes just "Notes." The citations on the page are listed numerically in the order in which they appeared in the text of the research paper.

Formatting Your Notes

When you use footnotes and endnotes, you label them with numbers. The first footnote or endnote in your paper is number 1. As you work through the paper, you progress in numerical order. In the body of your paper, this number should appear half a space above the last word cited. This placement is called *superscript*. There is no space between the last letter of the word or the period of the sentence cited and the superscript number.

A text reference to a typical footnote or endnote looks like this:

Harley-Davidson added an electrical starter to its motorcycles in 1965, and dubbed the new motorcycles the Electra Glide.[1]

At the bottom of the page where you inserted the reference to a footnote, you will show the citation for that note. Leave four lines between the last line of text and the first footnote. Indent five spaces from the left margin, and then start the citation with the number corresponding to the footnote. Leave one space after the number before you cite the source used.

The format of a footnote or endnote differs from a bibliography entry in that the note is shown as one complete sentence. Therefore, there is only one period in the citation, at the end of the sentence. The citation should show the author's full name with first name first, then a comma, the title of the source in italics, the city, publisher, and year of publication in parentheses, and the page number or numbers ending with a period.

The footnote citation for the previous example would look like this:

[1]Jim Lensveld, Harley-Davidson, *Factory and Custom Dream Machines* (London: Rebo Productions Ltd., 1992) 36.

If the footnote exceeds one line, do not indent any subsequent lines. There should be two line spaces between footnotes if there is more than one on a page. Endnotes follow a similar format, but are shown on the separate Endnotes page.

Use a full citation the first time that you reference a particular piece of work. If you reference the same piece of work in subsequent footnotes, use only the author's last name followed by the page numbers. A subsequent footnote citation for the preceding example would be shown simply as [2]Lensveld 48.

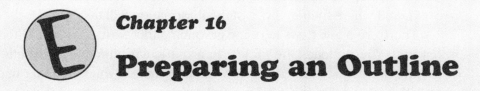

Chapter 16

Preparing an Outline

Once you finish gathering research, it is time to turn all those notes into a well-organized report. You will present your own analysis of the topic and blend it in with the facts and data that you researched. To do this effectively, you need to first prepare an outline. The outline keeps your paper flowing in a logical order and ensures that no important parts are missed.

Why Not Outline at the Beginning?

There are many reasons why you should outline after you finish doing your research. Many students try to do an outline for their project prior to doing any research. They can succeed at this to a certain extent if they already know their topic well, because they already have an idea about how to present it and where their analysis of the information will take them.

There are a few flaws to doing an outline this early, however. Often, the research you do leads the project in a particular direction. It is better not to have a preconceived notion of what information you will either need or find. If you have already done the outline, you may find yourself just looking for information that fits easily into your outline.

In addition, the further you get into your research, the more you might realize that you want to switch to a different kind of paper. You may have thought you would be writing an analytical paper, but find yourself uncovering little-known facts or obscure evidence. This may lead you to form a distinct opinion about your topic, thus prompting you to change to a persuasive paper. Though you are never tied to a rigid outline, there isn't much sense in doing the outline until you have a basic plan for your paper.

Know What Information You Have

Outlining after you research enables you to sort through the information you have, not the information you think you might have. It is much easier to take the notes you have made and sort them into groups than it is to try to figure out what groups there might be within your topic. You may find a significant amount of data available in an area for which you thought the data would be scarce. This area might also be divided into a few different subsections. The other extreme is possible as well. Your research could come to an abrupt halt if little or no information is available. By leaving the outline until after the research, you can tailor the paper to match the type and amount of information you find. The outlining process clearly shows you what you gathered through all the weeks you did your research. It helps you to figure out how to present your report in a clear and logical fashion that covers all aspects of your topic.

Refocus if Needed

Long before you reach the outline stage, you should have focused your research paper topic so that it is a single, well-defined subject. Once you begin to organize your notes, you may find that what you gathered is focused on a slightly different but related subject. You still can refocus your paper to reflect this. Because you are only now doing the outline, you can set it up to focus on any specific subject you want. Tailor the outline to suit the notes you have taken.

You should have a purpose or a main point that you are trying to prove with your research paper. All the sections in your outline should connect to this purpose. If most of them do not, you may need to adjust the purpose so that all of these sections will back it up.

Picking Out What Is Important

You generally will begin outlining by sorting out all the notes you have taken up to this point. While most of your notes should be consistent with your topic, some may no longer be suitable. Perhaps you changed the focus of your paper, or some things no longer seem to be worth including. Whatever the reason, this is the point at which you will organize and weed out your notes, keeping what is relevant and discarding what is not. You may even want to completely sort your notes at this point so you'll be ready to write your rough draft as soon as you complete your outline. Chapter 17 contains information about several systems that help you sort and organize your notes.

Facts

Most hard facts that are truly relevant to your topic will contribute toward the outline. This does not mean that you will present all of these facts in your final paper. For example, you will definitely include the facts that are necessary evidence to back up your position on an issue; you can leave out the facts that are simply extraneous statistics. For now it's a good idea to hold onto your notes on those facts because they are a solid indication of key ideas. When you have numerous facts relating to a specific area, that is likely to be an area that you should discuss in your research paper. You might not use the facts themselves in your paper, but the ideas surrounding them are important.

Information Supporting Your Focus

In reading through your notes you may find that while most are useful, some just don't fit the purpose of your paper. No matter how interesting or controversial, omit any information you gathered that is not relevant to your topic. If you find that some of your notes don't fit in any part of your outline, it may be that they are not applicable.

Be careful, though, that you aren't too quick to leave things out. Information that supports your main thesis is not always directly about your thesis. For example, suppose you are writing a research paper about a non-native species of fish that has taken over a local lake. You may not immediately see the benefit of including information about the discovery of a non-native tree frog in parts of the southern United States. However, this could be supporting evidence because it represents another example of how this problem crosses the boundaries of both species and geographical areas.

As long as your notes are relevant to your specific topic in some way, you should consider them when developing your outline. You usually can use the information that backs up your topic to decide what some of the sections of your outline should be about.

If you are not sure whether or not a note is pertinent, keep it. It is much easier to hang on to it now than it is to try to find the information again later if you decide you need it. Even if the information itself doesn't make it into your paper, you might want to refer to it at some point while you are writing. You can always discard it later if it doesn't fit in well enough.

Putting It in a Logical Order

After you decide what belongs in your report and what doesn't, figure out the order in which to present your information. There are a number of different ways to do this. The method you use depends both on personal preference and on the type of paper you are writing. It also depends on the topic you chose.

Chronological

Some topics, especially those with historical or timely information, make the most sense if they are organized in a chronological order. Begin with the oldest point that turned up in your research, and continue forward through time. In many cases, you will have not only some historical information, but also other information that doesn't fit into a timeline. Usually it is most reasonable to cover the historical information first, because it provides a good background or context for the subject. After that you can add the remaining information.

Background Information First

Any background information should be presented first so that the reader has an understanding of the topic before you delve into it deeper. Background information includes any basic details about the topic that are not common knowledge. Once you discuss this information, you can proceed, knowing that the reader has enough information to understand the rest of your paper.

ALERT!

Make sure you plan to include the data for each side of an argument with the information related to that side. Don't put information that belongs with an argument against the issue in the part of the outline that argues for the issue, and vice versa. This will only result in weakening both sides of the argument.

Present One Side First

If your paper deals with an issue or a debate that has two distinct sides, start by presenting one side. You may need to explain a few background details first if the topic is not well known or self-explanatory. Once you begin presenting one side, stay with that side until you have fully introduced it. Then you can present the other side. If your paper is a persuasive research paper, you will argue that one side is the correct one. You can present your side either first or second, whichever you think will give it the greatest impact.

Adding Your Own Analysis

The key part of a research paper is your own analysis of the topic. This can be a continuous analysis that carries on throughout the paper after you present the topic, or it can be an analysis that is added only in the latter part of the paper. Whichever way you decide to present your analysis is up to you. There is no right or wrong way to do it, and either way can work for most cases. Just be sure that you do add the analysis, because without it your paper will merely be a report.

Make Predictions

You can use the research you have to make predictions about your topic. Suppose you are writing a paper about an aspect of cloning. You might want to make some predictions based on your research. These could be about what society will think of cloning in the future, what problems will result from cloning, or what medical breakthroughs will occur as a result of what is learned about cloning. You must base your predictions on the research you have done. The predictions cannot come from your imagination; they must be deductions you have made because of what you have discovered and what you can now intelligently predict will happen.

ALERT!

When outlining a persuasive paper, you should find that you have at least a few different points to support your views. Your argument will be stronger if you arrange these points starting with the least important and ending with the most important or most powerful. If you do it the other way around, your argument will sound insubstantial and unconvincing.

Another way to analyze an issue is to debate for or against it. Using the same example of a paper about cloning, you could choose to argue either side. You could argue for it, stating that cloning is an important breakthrough that could lead to the treatment or maybe even the eradication of some diseases. On the flip side, you could argue against it, saying that it is morally wrong. You could say that developing the technology could lead to cloning for all sorts of criminal reasons. Whichever side you choose on any argument, you must present your case clearly. You must use concrete evidence and facts that you researched as the basis for your arguments, and you must clearly present the reasons why you feel the way you do.

Finding Gaps in Your Information

When you outline your paper, you may find that there are gaps in your information. For example, you may find that you don't have enough data and information to completely cover your topic. Lack of information usually becomes quite evident when you make your outline. If you can identify a section that belongs in your outline for which you have no notes, you need to fill that gap.

What you include in one section of your outline should lead into the next section. Though it is true that each section is a separate idea, there should be a logical order. If one step in the order is missing, the resulting paper will be choppy and disconnected.

Once you finish your outline, try to look at it objectively. In other words, if you were reading it for the first time, what questions would you have? Try to ensure that you are covering all aspects of your topic. Decide whether you are leaving out details about people, places, or things that are central to the topic. Similarly, determine whether you have left out any periods in a timeline, if that is applicable. Try to identify what is missing and what areas you don't have enough information about to round out the topic.

After you take a critical look at your outline, you may find you need to go back to do more research. This will be very focused research, because you know exactly what information you are missing and may be able to immediately pinpoint what the source of that information will be. If there are gaps in your information because the information is simply not available, you may need to draw your own conclusions. In this case it is very important that you make that distinction in your research paper and clearly note that this is not factual information, but is instead your own educated theory.

QUESTION?

Do I need an outline if the instructor doesn't require it?
Outlining is always a good idea. It helps immensely in organizing your notes before you write, helps you to construct your paper in a logical order, and identifies whether elements are missing or off topic. An informal outline without the proper format is better than no outline at all.

Formatting Your Outline

All of this emphasis and detail about what to include in your outline won't be very useful if you don't have a clear idea about what your outline should look like. If your instructor wants you to hand in your outline, she or he will usually have a specific format for you to follow. Formats can vary slightly, so make sure that you follow the one specified. If none is specified, use one of the ones presented here; they're the most common ways to outline any type of paper.

FACT

Most word processing programs have built-in outlining functions that will put your outline into the correct format for you. If you are using one of these programs, such as Microsoft Word, learn how to use this function. It will ensure that your outline is done properly and allows for easy revisions.

Outline Sections

When you organize your notes, you will find that they belong in a number of different categories, or sections. Each of these sections will make up a separate section in your outline, and ultimately a separate section in your research paper. Within each section there probably are subsections. Each subsection contains a different key idea about that section, and will become a paragraph or a few paragraphs in your research paper.

What each category includes depends solely on the topic of your research paper. A paper dealing with a well-known terrorist might chronicle the events in his life leading up to the point when he began committing acts of terrorism. Each significant part of his life might be a separate category. A paper dealing with combating the rising number of runaway street kids in big cities could have categories describing where these kids come from, why they leave home, what they do for food and shelter, agencies that exist to help them, and so on.

FACT

There are two types of outlines. One is a topic outline, which uses short bulleted items to list the topics that are covered in each section or subsection. The other type is a sentence outline, which uses complete sentences ending in a period to describe each section or subsection in more detail.

Numbering

You can use one of several different formats for numbering each section and subsection in your outline. Traditional outline numbering follows a specific format of letters and numbers. First, number the main sections with Roman numerals (I, II, III, and so on). Use capital letters (A, B, C, and so on) for the first level of subsections under the Roman numerals. If there is a further level of subsections after that, use Arabic numerals (1, 2, 3, and so on). In the event that there is still another level after that, use lowercase letters (a, b, c, and so on). For instance, your outline on the social class structure of ancient Rome might look like this:

I. Citizens
    A. Patricians
        1. Landowners
        2. Politicians
    B. Merchants and military officers
    C. Commoners
        1. Farmers
        2. Traders
II. Noncitizens
    A. Slaves
    B. Provincials

Another less common method of numbering uses numbers and decimals. This method is used most often in technical documents. To use this method, number the first section with the numeral 1 followed by a decimal point (1.). Add another decimal place to the first subsections, making them 1.1, 1.2, 1.3, and so on. Then add another decimal place for the next level of subsections. For example, the next subsections under 1.1 would be 1.1.1, 1.1.2, 1.1.3, and so on. Using this method, the same project represented in the preceding outline would like this:

1. Citizens
    1.1 Patricians
        1.1.1 Landowners
        1.1.2 Politicians
    1.2 Merchants and military officers
    1.3 Commoners
        1.3.1 Farmers
        1.3.2 Traders
2. Noncitizens
    2.1 Slaves
    2.2 Provincials

Indenting Your Outline

To make the outline even more clear and easy to follow, align each section to the left of the paper. Indent each subsection, with every subsequent subsection indented more. For example, an outline for a research paper on genetically modified foods might begin like this:

I. Advantages of GM foods
    A. Pest resistance
    B. No cost of chemical pesticides
    C. No health danger to consumers
    D. Resistance to drought
    E. Resistance to poor soil

The next heading in this example would of course be numbered II. and aligned to the left-hand side of the paper. You can see how the numbering and indenting makes it easy to identify where you are in the outline. This helps you once you begin turning those notes into paragraphs.

Chapter 17

Organizing Your Notes

You probably took some time to sort through your notes so you could make up your outline. Now you need to sort your notes into the right sections so that you can write the first draft. In fact, you might find it easiest to organize your notes as you prepare your outline. However you choose to do it, it is very important that you do sort through them all. You have invested far too much time already to leave out any vital parts.

Using a Chart

There are a few different methods that you can use to organize your notes. One method involves making a chart. Your chart might be one that covers an entire wall, or one that only covers a standard-sized piece of paper, depending on the amount of notes you took. The main point is to allow enough room to divide your notes into distinct sections. Then, when you write the paper from your notes, you simply look at one section of your chart at a time.

How to Use a Chart

You need a chart big enough to hold all your notes. If you first spread your notes out, you can make an estimate as to how big the chart has to be. On this chart, write headings for each of your sections. Then place your notes under the appropriate headings. You can do this in one of two ways. You can rewrite all of your notes onto the chart in the proper sections, or simply glue the notes onto the chart. Gluing is easiest if you used index cards, but it is still possible if you wrote your notes on regular sheets of paper. Because you only wrote on one side of the paper, you can cut out each note and glue it to your chart. It can be helpful to draw a thick line between sections so that when you begin writing the first draft, there is no confusion about where a note belongs.

QUESTION?

Can I use a chart to record my notes right from the beginning?
Yes, but you would need to have some prior knowledge of where the research would take you. You would need to either set up sections ahead of time, or pick out what they would be as you research. This is tricky, but it can be done.

If you took all of your notes on the computer, it is still possible to use the chart concept. Simply print your notes, cut out each one, and glue them onto the chart. This can be preferable to organizing your notes on the computer because it is easier to see the entire project at once. Students who are more visually oriented often have difficulty with organization if they can only see what is shown on one computer screen at a time.

Pros and Cons

Using a chart has its advantages and disadvantages. Writing the actual paper can be quite a straightforward process with a chart in front of you. You have all the similar ideas for one section right there. You can see what other sections you have, so you can set up the paper to progress from one section to the next. It is also easy to stay on topic if you have a constant reminder of what the other sections will cover. Following the chart ensures that you won't begin discussing something that belongs in another section.

On the down side, creating a chart is a time-consuming process, particularly if you recopy all of your notes. Even if you glue the index cards or cut-out notes onto your chart, it still takes many hours to organize your notes this way. It also takes up a lot of space, not only to create the chart in the first place but also to lay out the chart so you can use it to write your paper.

Using Index Cards

Index cards are not just for recording notes. Because each note is written on one index card, you can easily segregate and rearrange them. You can use the index cards themselves to organize the notes so that you can write the first draft of the research paper directly from them.

Some people find it easiest to shuffle or otherwise mix up their index cards before they start to sort them out. This ensures that notes from the same source won't ended up grouped together. It is one simple way to ensure that you give your paper a fresh approach to your topic.

How to Use Index Cards

If you decide to use index cards to organize your notes, you basically just sort them into groups or piles. Each group or pile consists of all the cards that have notes pertaining to a specific section. It is easy to gather all the similar cards together in the first place, and this method helps you figure out where a card goes should you misplace it.

Pros and Cons

With this system there is no rewriting of notes and no gluing. All you need to do is sort and organize. While you do need enough space to lay the cards out, they will soon be in smaller piles for each section. Then even if you spread out one pile at a time while you write your first draft, you will not need a lot of space. Also, after you have the cards split up into different sections, it is easy to arrange them within each section. They should progress in a logical order, and you can try different arrangements until you find the one that works best.

However, index cards are not without their problems. It is difficult to keep them in nice, tidy piles until you are ready to use them. You may drop them or shuffle them around by accident, and then you have to sort them out once again. The best way to prevent this is to secure each pile with an elastic band or a large clip so that the cards cannot become disorganized.

Numbering/Highlighting System

Another method of organizing notes is to use a numbering or highlighting system. These are actually two different systems, but you use them the same way. For this method you use notes that are on index cards or regular sheets of paper, and again there will be no copying and no gluing.

How to Use a Numbering/Highlighting System

In this system, you assign each section of your outline a different number or color. As you go through your notes, you decide which section each note belongs in. Then you either jot down the corresponding number beside the note, or you highlight the note with the correct color of highlighter pen. You could also just highlight the first word, or simply draw a line beside the note in the matching color. An entire sheet of notes highlighted with different color pens can be a little hard on the eyes.

For example, you might be writing a research paper titled "Personal Safety Devices and Why Some People Shun Them." You may have taken notes on personal safety devices such as seat belts, bike helmets, and sunscreen. Each one of these then becomes a separate section. When you are sorting through your notes, you might assign the number 1 to seat belts, the number 2 to bike helmets, and the number 3 to sunscreen. As you read over each note, you decide which section those notes belong in and write the appropriate number beside the note. You would use much the same method if you were using highlighter pens. You might assign blue to seat belts, pink to bike helmets, and yellow to sunscreen. You then would color each note with the corresponding highlighter.

Pros and Cons

This is another quick method of organizing notes. With just one look at all your notes, you should be able to label them with the correct number or color, and you don't need any more space to organize these notes than you need to store them. But while these are distinct benefits, there are a number of drawbacks to this system.

The main disadvantage is that once the notes are all labeled, this system is cumbersome to work with. You have to searching for the notes with the similar labels before you can begin writing each section. You may overlook some notes. It is difficult to write each section in the best order because you will be flipping back and forth from one note to the next. If you decide to use highlighter pens, you need to have as many different colors as you have sections. In a longer project, this may not be possible.

Organizing Notes on the Computer

You can use the computer to organize your notes. You are most likely to use a word processing program for this purpose, but you could also use a spreadsheet of some kind. The idea is to use the computer in much the same way as you would use a chart.

How to Use the Computer

The way you use this system depends largely on the type of program you use, your own level of expertise with the computer, and your own preferences. In general, you will type your notes onto the computer, either into a separate file for each section or under separate headings within one file. If you are fortunate enough to have a laptop, you may have put your notes directly on the computer in the first place. If this is the case, you now need to just cut and paste them so that they are all listed under the proper headings.

ALERT!

You can make use of your word processing program's outlining function when you add your notes. Simply type your notes directly into the section of the outline where they belong. Then, as you write your paper from your outline and notes, you will be able to see exactly where you are at any time.

Pros and Cons

Many people like the neat notes they end up with by typing them into the computer. You can easily move the notes to another section if you change your mind about where they best fit. If you come up with ideal phrasing for your paper while you are in the process of copying your notes, you can type that phrasing right in. That way it is there and can be placed directly into your research paper when the time comes. Of course, if you are working on a computer, take extreme care to back up all of your files.

QUESTION?

What should I do with notes that fit into more than one section?
This probably just means that you put too much information into one note. Use whatever system you have chosen to show which multiple sections the information fits into. Label those notes with two colors of highlighter, for example. Then make sure that the right information from that note gets into each corresponding section.

On the other hand, some people may find it difficult to work with their notes once they are on the computer. If you are typing your research paper on the computer, you need to be at ease with switching from one screen to another because both your file of notes and the file that contains the actual paper will be open. Many people find that this is difficult and prefer to write from notes that are on paper.

Another disadvantage to this method is the typing that you need to do in the first place. Typing all the notes that you spent weeks gathering will be quite time consuming.

Information That Doesn't Fit Anywhere

Unfortunately, not all of your notes will fit easily into a section of your outline. There will always be some notes that don't fit in anywhere. Then you have to figure out what to do with those notes based on their relevance and their quantity.

First you need to determine if each note is truly necessary to your research paper. Is it directly related to your topic? Does it add something to the paper that would be missed by its omission? Students often take notes that are too extensive, failing to stay focused on their narrowed topic or taking notes that either are too vague or are common knowledge. Such notes may not have a place in your research paper. You have to look at each note objectively to decide if it should be kept. If you decide to keep a note, you can add it in to the most closely related section. On the other hand, if you decide that a note is not truly relevant to your topic, you should discard it.

For example, your research paper topic could be "Cellular Phones: Should Everyone Have One?" You have divided your notes into sections on car accidents, personal safety, annoyances, health risks, and cost. Then in your notes you find an item that states "new technology will enable users to access news from their cell phones." This note doesn't fit in directly with any of the sections you have, but you believe it fits in well with your topic because it brings up a point you want to make about developing cell phone technology. You want to discuss cell phone capabilities that will be commonplace in the future and will be a benefit to everyone. For this reason you do not want to discard this note. After a while you decide that you could fit it into the section on cost. Your reasoning is that the future benefits of cell phones will outweigh the cost of having one.

Sometimes a few of your notes don't fit anywhere but are related to each other. In this case, it makes sense to create a new section in your outline. Once you do that, go back through all the other sections to see if any other notes fit better in the new section. Often you will find more.

Sometimes you will come across a note that you believe is central to your research paper. However, it doesn't fit into any section that you have and there are no similar notes to put into a new section. You may have to go back and do still more research. However, if the note is that important, this may be an area for which you can use your own analysis and interpretation. That may be enough to complete an entire section based on just one note.

Don't throw out any notes, including those you don't think you'll use, until after your paper is marked. Not only might you find a need for these notes when you actually write the paper, but you may want to refer to them again when you see your final grade and your instructor's comments, in case you need to clarify or fix anything.

Organizing Each Idea in Sequence

No matter which method you used, your notes are now organized into sections. However, there is still no logical sequence to your notes. They are bundled with other similar notes, but they are not yet ready for you to turn them into paragraphs. The following sections guide you through the process of turning those unconnected notes into a research paper you can be proud of.

When you organize your notes into sequence, you may come up with ideas for joining those notes together. Be sure to jot down those ideas as they come to you. Write them beside the notes, whether they are on index cards, a chart, or a computer file.

Follow Your Outline

If you finished your outline prior to organizing your notes, you can now follow the outline. It is organized so that your resulting paper will follow some sort of order. Whether it will be in chronological order, or present one side of an argument first, or be in a completely different order, you have already put some thought into making it flow logically. You can now put your sections of notes into the same order as your outline.

Of course, it is perfectly acceptable to change your outline whenever you see a way to improve it. You may find that a certain section flows more logically into a different section than you had originally planned for it. This may become much more evident once you take a close look at all of your notes. Make the necessary changes so that you will end up with a better paper. Even after you decide how the sections will be organized, consider another possibility to ensure that you haven't overlooked anything.

Take your time when organizing each section into sequence. This may seem like a simple task, but failing to do it carefully will make a major difference in the readability of your research paper. If it is not done well, your paper will be disjointed and confusing.

Organize Within Each Point

The sections that you came up with are not yet organized. Each section contains a complete idea or topic, but within the section there are a number of related notes in no particular order. You need to organize those notes using the same considerations that you used to organize your outline. If each idea follows a timeline, start at the beginning and work through the idea chronologically. Present background information before new thoughts and ideas. Group similar information together so that the thoughts flow continuously. Make sure that any major points are made toward the end of a section; this makes for a stronger paper. After you complete the process of creating an outline and following it with organized notes, you are ready to tackle the paper itself, which is the subject of the next chapter.

Reviewing Your Notes

You have just finished with writing, outlining, and organizing your notes. So why do you need to review them again? It is always a good idea to look over what you are about to write before you begin to write it. When material is fresh in your mind, you won't have to constantly check back to your notes as you write. If possible, take a break from your paper for a day or two before you write the first draft. It is nice to have a break from the intensity of the research you have done, and often this gives you a new perspective on your topic. Expect to make changes in your research paper between the time you write the first draft and the time you complete your project. Sometimes you can complete it in two drafts, but often it will take more. In the first draft, you want the writing process to be as natural as possible, so that what you want to say forms in your mind as quickly as you can get it down on paper. Review all your notes first, and then look over each section one more time when you read through the paper.

Avoid Repetition

Each part of your paper should include new and unique ideas. You don't want to repeat something that you already said in a previous section. As you review your notes, you may find notes and ideas that are the same, or at least very similar. Make sure that they are not an exact repetition. If there is a good reason why you need to use the same notes in more than one place in the paper—for instance, if you use them in a different context or as part of an example—make certain the information is worded differently when you write. Otherwise, you need to decide which place makes more sense and omit the other reference to the same note.

ALERT!

If possible, allow enough time to write your first draft in one sitting. It is easiest to avoid repeating yourself if you write the entire paper at once. If you do need to do it on separate days, reread what you have already written before you continue writing. Then the first part of the paper will be fresh in your mind.

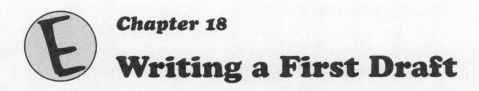

Chapter 18

Writing a First Draft

Finally you have reached the point that this whole exercise is about. You've already completed the hardest part of a research paper—choosing a topic, researching, taking notes, outlining, and organizing. All that is left now is to write the paper. You won't be able to produce a polished paper in your first try, so your tasks right now are to get the first draft down on paper using all those notes you took, keep it in a logical order using your outline and your note organization system, and then turn it into a research paper that is unique to you.

Be Clear About Your Purpose

Every part of your paper should reflect back to its purpose. Is there a question you are trying to answer? Is there a point you are trying to prove? Is there a new discovery you have made? This purpose is usually referred to as the thesis, and it is the basis of your entire paper. The notes you are now reviewing should all be a part of this purpose.

Your thesis needs to be completely clear to you in order for you to define that purpose clearly to the reader. While some of the discussion in your research paper may cover related areas of your topic, make sure there is always a point to those digressions. Each point should always lead back to your thesis and provide some sort of detail that aids the reader's understanding.

A research paper needs to strike a balance between including enough detail but not overexplaining things. Don't repeat yourself or stray off topic. On the other hand, don't leave out important points or miss basic information. Stay with the focus of each paragraph and include all the necessary detail.

The Thesis Statement

The thesis statement is often the one aspect of a research paper that causes students the most trouble. Yes, it is a very important part of the research paper, but students get very stressed out about getting their thesis statement perfected. While it is good to have such high ideals, the thesis statement is not that difficult to write. In fact, when you began this project by narrowing the focus of your topic, you came very close to defining your thesis statement.

What Is a Thesis Statement?

The thesis statement is usually a single sentence, although it could be two sentences. If it is not at the very beginning of the final research paper, it will be very close to the beginning. This statement organizes the purpose of the research paper. It tells the reader what the paper is all about. This statement is helpful to both the writer and the reader. It is there to keep the paper "on track" and to guide it whenever it starts to stray. While you collected research you probably referred back to the narrowed topic that you initially chose. What you were really doing was referring back to a form of your thesis statement. The thesis statement provides guidance to the reader in much the same way that it provides guidance to you as you research and write the paper. It is a reminder of the point you are trying to make with your paper.

Qualities of a Good Thesis Statement

A good thesis statement is a well-written, well-thought-out version of your narrow, focused topic. To ensure that your thesis statement is clear, use specific language. Readers should know exactly which statement is the thesis statement when they read your paper. If the thesis is well stated, it will stand out as an exact and precise statement, not a general one. The thesis statement can be controversial, and in fact it will pique the reader's interest if it is. You may state something that is the opposite of a commonly held belief, or something that others feel is wrong. This type of controversy, if it fits your topic, will add interest to your research paper. For instance, suppose you write this statement: "Exercise and social interaction have as much of a positive effect on clinical depression as do antidepressant drugs." This is a strong thesis statement that takes a stand, states your position clearly, and invites some controversy. If you write "Exercise and social interaction and how they compare to antidepressant drugs," you just leave your readers confused. The latter statement doesn't take a position; it only vaguely refers to some of the topics you discuss.

To be successful, the thesis statement must be strong and assertive about the conclusions you reach from your research. Don't sound as if you are unsure whether you can actually prove your thesis. Remember too that your thesis needs to be within the scope of your research. Don't get carried away and claim more than you can prove. Finally, state just one idea in your thesis, not two or more. Leave the others for another research paper.

Limit Each Idea to One Paragraph

Although it's usually obvious where a paragraph should end, sometimes you may be unsure. A good rule to follow is to keep each idea in one paragraph. Don't take more than one paragraph to cover an idea, and don't introduce new ideas in that paragraph. Of course, each paragraph leads into a closely related idea in the next one. You should be able to go back to any paragraph that you write in your research paper and summarize the idea of that paragraph in one brief sentence. This does not necessarily mean that every note you took will be discussed in one paragraph. Sometimes more than one note is about the same idea, and sometimes a note is so complex that it takes more than one paragraph to discuss it fully.

Keep Paragraphs Focused

Students make two common mistakes when writing paragraphs. One is letting the paragraph stray from its topic. Keep in mind what each particular paragraph is about while you write it. If you want to introduce a new idea, start a new paragraph. The other error is neglecting to expand on an idea. A well-crafted paragraph includes all the relevant data and explanation that you have for that particular idea. In other words, say everything that you have to say about that specific idea within that paragraph. If you keep your focus on the thesis statement as you write, the reader should be able to understand how each paragraph relates back to the main idea of your paper.

Follow your outline as much as possible while you are writing your paper. However, don't feel strictly bound to that outline. If something new occurs to you or if you see a better way of organizing while you are writing, make the necessary changes.

QUESTION?

How can I include an example without straying from the topic?
An example that is focused on that paragraph's topic does not stray from the topic. As long as it is relevant, an example can be very useful. It should not go into unnecessary detail, however. It is an illustration of the topic, not a creative writing exercise.

Provide Paragraph Transitions

Once you reach the point at which you are ready to discuss a new idea, begin a new paragraph. You should always logically connect the paragraphs to one another. Generally, the last sentence of a paragraph can provide a transition to the next paragraph. This keeps your writing from sounding choppy and disjointed, and holds the reader's interest.

You also can start a new paragraph if you shift gears to discuss a change in time. For example, if you are working through a timeline of events, the new paragraph could indicate the start of a year or any other segment in time that is significant to your topic.

A new paragraph also can indicate a change in location. If, for instance, your research paper includes a section about government subsidies for unemployed people, you may want to discuss this on a global basis. Therefore, you could have separate paragraphs describing the situation in the United States, in Canada, and in the United Kingdom.

You also should start a new paragraph whenever you introduce new people into the paper. If your paper deals with an issue that has affected several people, for example, and you tell their stories or interview some of them, you should begin a new paragraph each time you start to talk about a new person. You might discuss each one of them in a separate paragraph, or you might write several paragraphs about each person.

Including Your Own Views

Always remember that the key element of a research paper is that it includes your own views on the topic. It is important that this element make up a major portion of your paper all the way through. Some people find it easiest to first write the paper with just the data and facts they researched, returning to it afterward to add their own views wherever they are applicable. You might find this a cumbersome way to write, preferring instead to include your views the first time you put it all down on paper. Whichever way you write it, remember that this is just a first draft. The idea is to get everything written down. Don't make the mistake of trying to correct errors and perfect your prose as you write this draft. Nobody ever writes a perfect first draft. There will be time enough for revisions and editing later.

New Ideas

If you think of new ideas that are related to your topic, include them in the draft. Make sure that these ideas are based on your research, and fully back them up with sound reasoning. Because you are just writing your first draft, your ideas aren't likely to be completely formed. You may not be able to describe them in great detail the first time you write them down. This is fine. Resist the urge to leave them out until you have fully thought them through; you may forget even a great idea if you don't write it down. It is better to include what you have for now, and then edit and change and rewrite later. Those first fresh ideas can be the strongest aspect of your paper.

ALERT!

If you find it difficult to think and type or write at the same time, you can dictate your paper into a tape recorder. Later, you can transcribe what you dictated. Some people find that their ideas flow easier through speech than they do through writing.

Personal Perceptions

You may also have your own perceptions to include in this research paper. Perceptions differ from ideas in that they are not something you form in your mind based on facts, but rather something you discern based on what you see or hear. Interviews that you conduct are a common source for your own perceptions. You may perceive something new because of the interviewees' body language or because something about their surroundings contradicts other facts you have uncovered.

Arguments

If you are writing a persuasive research paper, you need to include your own arguments. Develop these arguments fully, presenting your position and explaining your reasons for that position using facts you discovered during your research. It is not enough to just state your opinion. You need to explain the reasons why you feel the way you do, which includes discussing the possible consequences of that opinion and defending it against possible arguments.

Key Parts of a Paragraph

Your paper will comprise many different paragraphs, but they all will be structured in much the same way. Each usually begins with a topic sentence, followed by supporting details and a summary sentence that ends the paragraph. This is the same whether the paragraph is defining something, comparing two or more things, describing a series of events, or making judgments or evaluations.

The opening sentence introduces the ideas in that paragraph, revealing to the reader what the paragraph is about. It does not have to be a statement; it could be a question or an exclamation. In fact, some variety in your opening sentences will make your paper more interesting to read. Remember that the paragraph's main idea should be stated succinctly when the reader gets to the topic sentence.

The topic sentence can occur anywhere in a paragraph of your research paper. It is often the first sentence, but it does not have to be. It can also occur in the middle of a paragraph, and is sometimes most effective as the last sentence of the paragraph.

All of the other sentences in a paragraph should relate back to that first sentence in some way. They are there to support the idea and to add more detail to it. Take care to keep these supporting sentences focused on the main idea of the paragraph they are in. They should describe the idea more completely, use examples to further illustrate the idea, or explain the reasons for that idea.

Paragraphs can contain any number of sentences. Some paragraphs are only one sentence long, while others may be dozens of sentences long. Overly long paragraphs are difficult to focus and difficult to read, so most instructors suggest that paragraphs be limited to three to eight sentences.

The final sentence of each paragraph summarizes the thoughts of that paragraph. It is often just a restatement of the topic sentence using different words, and it is used to complete the main idea of the paragraph. The last sentence of a paragraph can also contain the suggestion of another related idea, which will be the topic of the next paragraph, of course.

Writing an Introductory Paragraph

Every research paper needs to have a well-crafted introductory paragraph. Because this paragraph is the reader's doorway into your paper, it needs to be strong and inviting. You want readers to be intrigued by both your topic and your stance on that topic, so make the wording clear and concise.

Your introductory paragraph should talk about concepts in the same order in which they are discussed in the body of the paper. If you introduce ideas in one order but later discuss them in a different order, your paper will be disjointed and potentially confusing. This is one reason why it is often easiest to write the introduction after you write the body of your paper.

ALERT!

Avoid beginning your paper with statements such as "This paper is about..." or "In this paper I will prove..." These sound awkward and do nothing to add to the flow of the paper. You can tell what your paper is about without announcing that you are telling what it is about.

Grab the Reader's Attention

The introductory paragraph should grab the reader's attention and make him or her want to read the rest of the paper. It can begin with a question that you will answer in your paper, a statement that you will either support or dispute, or even a shocking declaration that you might confirm. Research papers should begin in much the same way as a speech. If you start with something that immediately captures the attention and imagination of the audience, you have hooked them into reading more or listening to more.

State the Idea Clearly

As important as it is to grab the reader's attention, it is even more important to state the main idea, or thesis, of the research paper clearly and early. Work this main idea into the introductory paragraph.

Along with the thesis statement, the opening paragraph should contain enough related information to start the paper moving forward. This could include little-known facts, historical information, or a related story. Carefully connect this information with the thesis statement so that it doesn't slow down the paper with too much detail. Make sure that any information you include in the introductory paragraph is directly related to the main idea. In other words, you should have a clear purpose for stating information in the introductory paragraph.

For example, consider the following opening paragraph for a research paper about the benefits of adding fluoride to drinking water:

"There was a time when people didn't pay much attention to dental care until they had a toothache, so it may surprise you to know that cavities were fairly unusual. A closer look at the diets of these previous generations, however, offers some insight into the reasons for their healthy teeth: They didn't suck on mints, grab a quick cappuccino, or munch on doughnuts. In short, they ate a mainly healthy diet of whole foods. Now, most of us eat too many over-processed, sugary foods and pay the price for it with our dental health. There is hope, however, and it comes in the form of fluoride in our drinking water. Adding fluoride to our drinking water improves our dental health while posing no risk to our overall health." The thesis statement here is the last sentence of the paragraph, but the previous information drew the reader into the topic.

You do not have to write the introductory paragraph first and the concluding paragraph last. Sometimes it is easiest to write the body of the report first, and then figure out what to say in the introduction and conclusion. The only rule is that the final draft must be in the correct order.

Writing a Conclusion

You must have a concluding paragraph at the end of your research paper. Without a conclusion, your paper will be unfinished and will not fully resolve the thesis. The conclusion is almost always more than just a sentence. Generally it will take a full paragraph to wrap up the research you have presented. Refer back to your introductory paragraph, and finish what you began there.

If you asked a question in your introduction, answer it in your conclusion. You may even want to restate the question. That is an effective way to direct the reader's attention back to the purpose of the research paper. Make sure that you answer the question in full. Leave no portion of the answer unexplained.

Your conclusion needs to do just that: conclude. It needs to sum up what the introduction started. It should never be simply a restatement of your thesis, but instead should show how you have proven the thesis statement. The concluding paragraph can be a summary of what was in the paper, and it can also ask a question, make a comparison, or suggest some action.

One effective way to end a research paper is to make a prediction that is central to the topic. This prediction should follow logically from the information that you presented within the paper. For instance, suppose the topic of your paper were the start of a health-care crisis in your town because of a growing population of senior citizens. After presenting all your research, you might conclude with a statement such as "Local doctors will be available only to the seriously ill within the next five years unless enough new doctors can be convinced to move here." Make sure that any prediction you make is based on your research and backed up by the facts you presented in your paper.

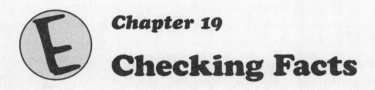

Chapter 19

Checking Facts

Once you finish the first draft, it is time to start polishing it. There are a few different tasks that you need to complete before your rough draft becomes your final draft. One of the first of those tasks is to check the accuracy of all the facts that you use in your paper. Even a small factual error can undermine the credibility of an entire paper.

Double- and Triple-Check!

You can do some of the fact checking during a simple read-through of the paper, because some errors are obvious. You need to do more than just a brief scan, however. Read through the paper at least two or three times. Read it once to yourself and then once aloud, as if you were reading it to someone.

Check for Typos

The most obvious errors are simple typos. These always find their way into your paper as you rush to get your ideas down, so there may be a number of these in a first draft. A common typo is something like writing "this is the newest feature on these cares" instead of "this is the newest feature on these cars." You didn't intend to type "cares," but that is the way it came out because you were typing quickly or because you mind had already moved on to what you were about to type next.

ALERT!

Don't rely on spell checkers to catch your typos. As long as what you have typed is an actual word (such as "cares," when you meant "cars"), the spell checker won't show that it is an error. You need to find most of the typos yourself. Take your time with this process, because it can mean the difference between presenting a well-polished paper and a sloppy, hastily put-together paper.

The easiest way to check for typos is to read your paper out loud. When you read it silently you can still skip over the typos, sometimes reading what you think is there instead of what is really written there. When you read it aloud you are forced to say the words the way they are typed, so the typos are much more evident. You also could ask someone else to read through your paper to check for typos. A fresh pair of eyes that is completely unfamiliar with the paper will catch any remaining typos quicker.

Ensure That It Makes Sense

At this stage you should also ensure that what you wrote is logical and makes sense. Again, there may be some obvious errors that will confuse the reader. These usually stem from facts that you either recorded incorrectly or were wrong at the source.

This brings up the possibility that not all of the sources you found were completely accurate. This is especially true with some Web sites, because there are no rules or guidelines regulating who can post information on the Internet and what that information contains. Check these facts with another source so that you get the correct facts.

Assessing Your Sources

While the focus in recent years has been on the inaccuracies of some Web sites, be aware that any source you use can contain inaccuracies. These may be errors that were printed in books or magazines because those writers didn't check their facts. They may be errors on maps or in atlases that reflect either mistakes or outdated information. If your information is from a personal interview, that too can contain incorrect information, either because the interviewee doesn't know the correct answer or doesn't want to disclose it. In addition, memories are extremely prone to error.

So how will you know if a source is reliable or not? When you use a source, consider who provided the information. Was it a professional researcher and writer? Was it a disgruntled former employee? Also consider the author's relationship to the topic. Knowing more about the source's author can sometimes help you gauge the reliability of the information that the source contains.

Find out how current the information is. An article or book that was published in the past six months is likely to contain information that supersedes the information provided in an article or book published fifteen years ago. In addition, the purpose of the publication can have an effect on the bias of the information it includes. Information that was published to convince or persuade people of a specific position may slightly skew the facts. In fact, any source that is opinion-based should be noted as such so that you can differentiate between opinions and facts. Finally, you should check the background and credentials of any person you receive information from.

People can forget details, they can mix opinions with facts, and they may not have known the correct information in the first place.

Verifying Quotes

You must be absolutely certain about details when you use quotes, whether the source is a person you interviewed or a written quote that you uncovered during your research. Because quotes are assumed to be exact, you need to ensure that all the details you have in your notes are precise as well. You can check quotes you gleaned from written sources by referring back to those same sources. You can check quotes that came directly from a person you interviewed or one you asked for information if you have a tape recording of your conversation. If you don't have a tape recording, you should be absolutely sure you that wrote down the person's responses word for word. If you are at all unsure, double-check with the person you are quoting.

All direct quotes must be enclosed in quotation marks. Place the quotation marks around the exact quote itself, which may be only part of a sentence if the rest is in your own words. Always immediately attribute the quote to the person who said it.

The wording of a quote must be exact. You cannot paraphrase any part of what was said and then pass it off as the words of others. You also cannot make any improvements to the quote if you think it could be worded better. If you feel it needs this, you can write your own explanation or clarification, but make sure you differentiate between the quote and your wording.

Keep your notes and tape recordings of any interviews you have conducted. Interviewees can dispute that they ever said what you recorded as a quote in your paper. If you have a tape recording as a backup, you can prove that you did in fact use an exact quote.

Make sure that you attribute any quotes to the people who said them. This may seem obvious, but is the cause of many errors. If you are talking to one person, it is very clear who should be quoted. But, if you are talking to a group of people, you need to make sure you know exactly who said what. Don't rely on your memory; write down who is responsible for each quote. If you are getting a quote from a book, it may be unclear who should be credited with the quote. Make sure you understand without a doubt who it was. If you can't be sure of who said it, don't use it as a quote at all. You can still use the information that comes from the quote, but instead put it in your own words.

Spelling of Names and Places

Always correctly spell names and place names that you use in your research paper. This can be difficult if they are misspelled at the source, so learn the correct spelling of names you are referring to by checking with official documents if they are available. Any legal documents will have names spelled properly. Encyclopedias are also a reliable source of proper spellings of names of important people. Remember that just because a name is commonly spelled one way does not mean that your subject spells his or her name that way. Your subject might be named Jesse, but it could just as easily be spelled Jessie or Jessy or Jessi or some other combination. No one likes to see his or her name spelled incorrectly, so be sure to get it right.

The one instance in which you may come across different spellings of the same name is when the name is translated from another language. If there is no English equivalent of some of the letters or sounds, many different spellings may be assumed to be correct. Choose the one you come across most often and use it consistently throughout your paper.

Place names are generally easier to track down. Despite the fact that they may be spelled incorrectly in some sources, they should always be correct on a map or in an atlas. Take the time to make sure you have it right. Proper spelling helps a paper look professional, whereas incorrect spelling detracts from a paper, calling into question other aspects of the writing.

Gender and Preferred Social Titles

It is also important to have a person's gender and preferred social title correct in your paper. Sometimes it is hard to know whether a person is male or female just by reading about the person. Referring again to the example used earlier, a person named Jesse could be of either sex. Unless the person is specifically referred to as either "he" or "she," or there is a photo that leaves no doubt, the reader won't know. Take care not to make any assumptions. Even a name that you assume to be clearly associated with one sex can actually refer to someone of the opposite sex.

When you directly quote a professional person, you should always ask that person how to refer to his or her job title. Don't assume that the person you think is the manager, for instance, will want to be referred to as the manager. People may have a more specific title that they would like you to use.

Always refer to people by their preferred social title. If in doubt, ask what it is. An unmarried woman is a Miss and a married woman is a Mrs., but either one might prefer to be a Ms. Remember that some women keep their maiden name when they marry, some take their husband's name, and some combine the two names with a hyphen. Some divorced women keep their married name; others return to using their maiden name. You could also get mixed up when professional titles are used. If you interview a doctor or a dentist, you know that person is referred to as "Doctor" (Dr.). However, you may not know that a retired person retains the title of Dr., or that someone with a doctorate in any field can use the Dr. designation.

FACT

You can use either the Dr. designation or follow the person's name with the abbreviation of his or her degree, such as M.D. or Ph.D. Do not use both at the same time. Use Dr. the first time you refer to someone with a doctorate degree, but use it in subsequent referrals only if that person's degree is in the field of medicine.

Be careful when you are referring to someone with a religious or military title. Is the minister you interviewed referred to as the Reverend Roberts or Father Roberts? Is the soldier you spoke to Corporal Davies or Sergeant

Davies? Never make any assumptions when it comes to titles. People will always be happier to tell you how to refer to them properly than they would be to see their names written incorrectly in your paper.

Towns, Cities, States, Countries

You can usually confirm the correct spelling of place names on a legitimate map or globe, but some places won't be shown there. A very small town will only be shown on a local map. A historical village that no longer exists will only be shown on historical maps. Take the time to ensure that you get this right at the word's first usage, and ensure that you always spell it right thereafter. Again, you can double-check these spellings by finding them in more than one reliable source.

Verifying Geographical Details

You now have the place names spelled correctly, but there still may be errors in other geographical details.

Get a map and check the location of any events you discuss in your paper. You may discover details that you didn't come across during your research that could make a huge difference to your paper. Maybe a location is on an island or very close to a major city or at the southernmost point of the state or country. These details could change the way you view certain aspects of your topic. You may also find that a certain location in relation to other locations either brings to mind some new ideas or highlights some errors. You may discover that the primary town in your paper is located at the junction of two rivers. Because of this you come up with some new theories that relate back to your paper's topic. For example, your research might indicate that a journey was completed in three hours, when actually it would take about three days. Other errors could include cities that were actually located within the boundaries of a different country during the years referred to in your paper.

You should check all relevant geographical data. Make sure that a city is really a city and not just a village. A local mountain that never receives any snow because of its location shouldn't be referred to as having snow-capped peaks. These types of details may seem obscure or trivial to you, but if someone reading your paper had actually been to the places you described, he or she would find it laughable. All of those little details are what give your paper its credibility.

What if I can't find any other sources to back up this information? Your best bet may be to ask a direct question of someone who obviously would know what's correct. If you need geographical information from a specific place, try asking the local tourism office for the precise information you need.

Historical Timelines

Students and other writers often have trouble with historical details. Because they may be writing about a period in time they didn't even live in, or at least have forgotten about, the exact details are hard to come by. With a little effort, you can ensure that your paper contains accurate information.

Ensure Internal Consistency

Because your facts came from many different sources, there is always the chance that one or more of those sources were incorrect, resulting in glaring errors. Suppose your paper has to do with historical emperors in China. One of your sources states that Pu-Yi became the last Manchu Emperor in 1908, when he was two years old. Another source states that this happened in 1937, when he was twenty-eight years old. Obviously one of these sources is wrong. Not only could Pu-Yi not become emperor in two different years, but the years and the ages don't add up. There are twenty-nine years between 1908 and 1937, but your research claims he only aged twenty-six years during that time. You will need to double-check these dates and ages with as many other sources as it takes to get it right. By the way, Pu-Yi did become the last Manchu Emperor of China in 1908 when he was two years old, but he was named Emperor of Manchukuo by the Japanese in 1934.

Here's another example. A paper that makes mention of a young man drafted into the army during the Vietnam War may also say that he graduated from high school in 1974. If you know that the United States pulled out of Vietnam in 1973, this fact does not make sense. One of the dates, quite possibly the graduation date, must be incorrect. As you read through your first draft, ask yourself if all the dates mesh together properly.

Some historical data simply does not exist. Other data may be confusing due to the way information was collected in the past. However, if there are photos pertaining to your topic, they will show you details you might not find elsewhere. Be sure to use this information whenever you can.

Confirm Other Historical Details

In addition to dates, any other historical details need to be reasonable. At different points in history people dressed differently, ate differently, used different modes of transportation, and lived in different types of shelters. You can't mix references to modern-day life with a historical paper any more than you would have people in today's society hitching their horse to the post in front of the saloon or putting on their petticoats and bonnets. Another common mistake is to introduce modern conveniences prior to their invention. At its most extreme, this can have almost comical results. You know that Paul Revere couldn't interrupt a television show for an emergency broadcast any more than Mozart could have taken up playing the bass guitar. Do some background research to ensure that you know what life was like during the period of time encompassed by your research paper.

Maintaining Timeliness

You probably spent a significant amount of time doing your research. During that time, some of your information may have become outdated. This may seem hard to believe, but certain things do change very rapidly. You should make sure you check your paper for this before you proceed so that all of your information will still be current.

Effects of Sources

The types of sources you use will have an impact on the timeliness of your information. Newspapers, magazines, and sometimes Web sites are the most current sources you can use. They often are published daily, so they have the opportunity to provide the most up-to-date coverage of a topic. Look at the dates on all of the sources that you used. If you use information from a Web site, you should look for a date there that shows when the information was last updated.

Because these sources are updated so frequently, they may make compromises in the depth of coverage they provide. They also are prone to errors, because there isn't enough time to thoroughly check out a story before it is printed. Books contain the least current information, but the most in-depth. A significant amount of time can pass between the time a book is written and the time it is printed, and then it will stay on a shelf for years afterward. Though some information in a book (such as historical facts) will never become outdated, more timely information (such as up-to-date statistics or trends) should come from a different, more current source.

Effects of Your Topic

Certain topic areas are likely to become outdated much more quickly than do others. Topics that involve the fields of science, technology, medicine, and some areas of business change rapidly. New developments and new discoveries could vastly change the facts you gathered. Be particularly cautious if your research paper discusses one of these fields. Events that have occurred since you began your research will change some facts you reported, and at their most extreme may affect your entire thesis.

Update Necessary Information

If you find that your information has become outdated, and the changes have a major impact on your paper, you should conduct more research into the areas that have changed. You may not be able to do this, though, if the new research will take a significant amount of time. There might not be enough time left to go through this process again. If your topic is one that changes that rapidly, you could find yourself continually trying to catch up to the latest changes. For example, a paper that includes information about casualties in Iraq would be hard to keep current.

Consider a Disclaimer

If necessary, you may use a disclaimer, which confirms that all of the facts were current as of the date you collected them. You can do this if you don't have the time to carry out more research to update your facts. You also can use a disclaimer if the facts are in such a continuous state of change that you know you can never keep up with them. Don't use a disclaimer to mask the fact that you just didn't want to bother finding more current information.

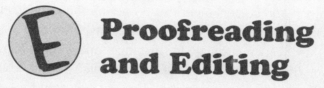

Chapter 20

Proofreading and Editing

Now you have reached the crucial point of polishing your first draft. The proofreading and editing process will take you from a rough draft to a final draft that shows your best work. During this process you probably will not change any of the content of your paper, but you will make changes in the wording and ensure that you are using proper English throughout. This is your opportunity to rewrite any sections that you didn't have the time to refine during the first draft.

Checking Spelling and Grammar

The spelling and grammar in a formal research paper must meet top standards. You can begin by using the spelling and grammar checker in a word processing program, but this should only be the start of the process. You still need to go through your paper word by word and sentence by sentence to ensure that you catch and correct all errors. Sometimes automatic checkers catch what can only be referred to as potential errors. They flag any words for spelling that they don't recognize, for instance, and almost all cases of passive voice, even though sometimes the passive voice is preferable. Make sure that you don't blindly agree to every change suggested by a spelling and grammar checker. Instead, use them merely as guidelines.

You need to slow down when you are doing any proofreading and editing. Read your paper word by word at a much slower pace than you would usually read. If you read at your normal pace, you will not see all of your errors.

Spelling

With so much advanced software available, you would think that a spell checker could find and fix any errors in your paper. However, no spell checker can recognize every word, and if you have ever used a spell check program before, you know how often it flags common words. One thing spell checkers often cannot do is identify places in the text where you have spelled a word correctly but have used the wrong word. That is why there is no substitute for your own proofreading, or someone else's.

You can speed up this process if you know what to look for. For example, it is common to make errors in pluralized words. This being the English language, there are as many exceptions to rules as there are rules themselves. Here are some rules to remember:

- For words ending in "s," "sh," "tch," "x," or "z," add "es," as in "messes" and "witches."

- For words ending in "ch" with a soft sound, add "es," as in "porches."
- For words ending in "y" preceded by a vowel, add an "s," as in "days."
- For words ending in "y" preceded by a consonant, change the "y" to an "i" and add "es," as in "countries."
- For words ending in "o," you usually just add an "s" to form the plural, as in "memos." In a few instances you add "es," as in "potatoes."
- For words ending in "f," you usually change the "f" to a "v" and add "es," as in "elves." In some cases you add an "s" to make the word plural, as in "beliefs."

Proofread and edit for different errors each time you read through your paper. Don't try to catch everything with one pass through it. You should also save the edited draft after each round of corrections in case you want to go back to a previous draft at any point.

You also need to pay close attention to possessives. In most cases it is a simple enough rule to add an apostrophe and an "s" to a noun to make it possessive. When the noun is singular and ends with the letter "s," you add an apostrophe and an "s." When the noun is plural and ends with the letter "s," you just add an apostrophe. When you are writing the possessive of a family name, you make it plural first, and then just add an apostrophe. Therefore, the possessive of the name Spalding is Spaldings'. Possibly the most important rule is to stay consistent throughout your paper and show these possessives the same way every time.

One of the most common errors with possessives occurs with the words "its" and "it's." "Its" is the possessive form of the word, whereas "it's" is a contraction of "it is."

Word Usage

As you proofread, check for proper word usage. As you read through the paper, look out for words that are frequently mistaken for similar words, or for words that don't fit the context of the sentence. These could be words that you used despite being unsure of their meaning. When you write the first draft you know what you want to say, but you can't find the correct words to use. Because you are writing quickly, you put down the best word that you can think of at the time. When you proofread the first draft those words should catch your eye because the meaning of the sentence will be a bit jumbled. This also can happen if you try to make your paper sound more academic than it needs to be. You should use formal English, but not to excess.

Some similar words that are often confused and used improperly include these:

Common Errors in Word Usage			
First Word	**Meaning or Usage**	**Second Word**	**Meaning or Usage**
Accept	receive or agree to	Except	not including
Advice	a recommendation	Advise	to offer advice to
Affect	to influence or cause a change in	Effect	to bring about; a consequence
Council	group meeting for discussion	Counsel	to advise; advice or guidance
It's	contraction of *it is* or *it has*	Its	possessive form of *it*
Lose	fail to keep	Loose	not tight
Principal	most important; a sum of money	Principle	moral rule
Saw	used after a noun or pronoun	Seen	used after a helping verb such as *have*

Capitalization

Errors in capitalization almost never change the meaning of the sentence, but they are a distraction to the reader and indicate a lack of effort on the writer's part. Check with *The Chicago Manual of Style* or whatever style guide you are told to use to verify your capitalization. These are some of the main capitalization rules to remember:

- Capitalize the first word of every sentence.
- Capitalize the first word of long quotations that are set off.
- Capitalize all names of people.
- Capitalize the days of the week and the months of the year.
- Capitalize the names of holidays.
- Capitalize the main words in a title, but not prepositions, articles, or conjunctions.
- Capitalize place names and country names.
- Capitalize the points of a compass.

Punctuation

You can easily check your punctuation by reading each sentence separately. Don't try to read through the paper in sequence while checking for punctuation. You need to do this very slowly, one sentence at a time. Use exclamation marks and question marks very sparingly, if at all. Your research paper should not "shout" to the reader or pose questions. In a research paper you make statements, which means that most sentences can end in a period.

The more common errors come with some of the other types of punctuation, and you should always confirm the correct punctuation rule with the style guide you are using. Here are a few brief guidelines:

- Use commas after every item in a list and before a joining word in a long sentence. ("The top spice exports from India include pepper, turmeric, ginger, and cardamom.")
- Use quotation marks at the beginning and end of every direct quote. ("Mr. Whitby said, 'The food was very bland, lacking completely in spice of any kind.'")
- Use colons to introduce lists. ("You will need the following materials: an old tie, some polyester stuffing, and four small pieces of felt.")
- Use semicolons to link two complete but related sentences. ("He had very large feet; his shoes had to be custom made.")
- Use parentheses, or brackets, to separate a group of words from the rest of a sentence. ("The dog (a Rottweiler) had ten puppies gathered around her.") Use brackets when you want to put parentheses

inside parentheses. Some citation styles require the use of angled brackets around e-mail or Web site addresses.

- Use hyphens to form some compound words. ("She was their key decision-maker while only in her mid-twenties.")

People usually have difficulty with one or more specific types of punctuation. Concentrate on catching those, but watch for others as well.

Common Grammatical Errors

Though automated grammar check in a word processing program picks up some errors, it also skips many of them, and frequently flags items that are fine. It is up to you to check for grammatical errors. While there are a multitude of grammatical errors, some are more common than others. Check the style guide to confirm the proper grammatical form. You may also want to check a guide that focuses on grammar, such as *Grammatically Correct,* by Anne Stilman, or *Elements of Style,* by William Strunk, Jr., and E. B. White.

ALERT!

Most people tend to make the same mistakes repeatedly. These may be certain grammatical errors, words you always misspell, or words you commonly misuse. Take note of these mistakes, and watch for them specifically whenever you proofread a paper.

Students quite often use a comma to join two independent clauses. You should use either a period or a semicolon to join these. For example, it is correct to state "We camped at this spot often; it was secluded yet close to everything we wanted." Papers also often contain sentence fragments and run-on sentences. A sentence fragment is only part of a sentence. If it were read by itself without the sentence before or the sentence after, it would make no sense. All of your sentences need to be complete. A run-on sentence is one that could easily be split into two or more complete sentences. It contains no punctuation to indicate any pause when it is being read. It should be split up into as many complete sentences as possible.

Avoid wordiness. Sometimes students also use sentences that go on and on explaining something that could be explained in a simple, direct method. Some examples and descriptive language help to fully explain a thought, but you should keep the focus in your sentence and avoid rambling. Also, make sure that all of the subjects and verbs are in agreement. This means that they are either singular or plural, not a mixture of the two, and that they are both referred to in the first person, second person, or third person. For instance, use "The girls dressed up in costumes from the Renaissance," not "The girls dressed up in a costume from the Renaissance."

A final common grammatical error is the misplaced modifier, which causes misinterpretation of the entire sentence. For example, if you state that "The car barely missed the old cow as it sped across the field," you are suggesting that the cow is speeding across the field, not the car. A better construction would be "The car sped across the field, barely missing the old cow." The modifier should always appear as close as possible to the words it is modifying. Then there will be no confusion as to what it is modifying.

Achieving Clarity

Your writing will be much easier to read if you strive for clarity. If you find that you are rereading a section several times to get the meaning, you are probably using wording that is not clear enough. If it is not clear to you, it will certainly not be clear to someone who is not as familiar with your topic.

Avoid Shortcuts

Try not to use abbreviations or acronyms, even if you think they are commonly known. The reader might be unfamiliar with these shortcuts and not know what you are talking about from that point on. Write out the names or words in full the first time you use them in your paper, and add the common abbreviation in parentheses. You can use the abbreviated form after that. Similarly, always include a person's first name at the first reference to that person, no matter how famous. For example, in a paper about evolution, you would identify Charles Darwin or Alfred Wallace by their full names the first time you referred to them, although "Darwin" and "Wallace" would be acceptable, respectively, after that.

Avoid Figures of Speech

Figures of speech liven up a creative piece, but there is no place for them in a research paper or any other technical writing. These include phrases such as "the car is a gem" or "the results broke the scales." While there is no harm in using a metaphor here or there, you should try not to continually use any kind of figure of speech very often in your writing. It will only confuse your reader.

Use Words You Understand

Using words you don't understand always has the potential to get you in trouble. Sometimes you think you know the correct meaning of a word, but you use it in the wrong context. A word used incorrectly can twist the entire meaning of a sentence. If the word is uncommon, readers might not know the meaning of it, and you might get away with using it the wrong way. On the other hand, they very well may know the meaning of a word you used incorrectly, and that would reflect very poorly on you. Use your own natural vocabulary in your paper, without trying to sound more "academic" or "sophisticated."

Don't Overexplain

Some students have a tendency to go into great detail explaining things. They use four sentences to get a point across when one or two would be enough. The best rule to remember is to *keep it simple*. When you proofread, keep an eye out for explanations that seem to go around in circles. If a point can be expressed in twenty words, don't use forty.

Vary Sentence Structure

A paper that is written with variety is much easier to read. Vary your sentence structure so that the sentences are of differing lengths. If you use short sentences all the time, your paper will sound choppy. If you use long sentences all the time, you will lose the reader in the long details.

You should also try to start your sentences with different words. Five sentences in a row starting with the word "I" is monotonous to read, and will detract from what you are trying to say. Reword your sentences so that they say the same thing but begin with different words.

Stay Positive

Try to keep your writing positive. You wouldn't want to read a paper in which every sentence begins with "Don't" or "Never." Again, this is simply a matter of rewording the sentences. Change your stance from explaining what should not be done to explaining what should be done. This is psychology that most parents understand very well!

Avoid Slang and Clichés

Try not to use any slang terms, jargon, or shortened modern language in a formal research paper. This includes the type of spelling that you might use in an e-mail or on an Internet forum, such as tonite, gonna, FYI, or LOL. You should also keep contractions to a minimum, so that instead of writing *couldn't*, for example, you would write *could not*. Clichés sound unique and original when they are first used, but they quickly become tiring, such as "think outside the box" or "at the eleventh hour." After a while, these expressions lose any impact. Come up with your own way of describing or expressing something to avoid using clichés.

Read It Out Loud

Once you have read through your paper and corrected all the spelling and grammatical errors, go through it again, reading out loud. Errors become much more evident when you speak the words rather than reading silently. Pay close attention to what you are saying while you read. By this time you have corrected the more obvious errors; the ones that remain will be harder to spot.

FACT

Reading your paper out loud helps so much with proofreading because you are using two of your senses. When you read silently, you only use sight to catch any errors. However, when you read out loud not only do you use sight, but you also hear the words. The two senses combined are more proficient at spotting errors.

Any words that are missing or incorrect will be quite evident as you read out loud. While you did check for this earlier, you will have made many changes since then. New errors can crop up, either due to new things that you typed in or revisions that changed the sentences. Read through the entire paper to ensure that all the words are there and that they are used and spelled correctly.

Avoid repetition. While your sentences and paragraphs may all be correct now, they still may not be the easiest to read. Most of us have a tendency to reuse the same wording over and over again. Your paper will read much more smoothly if you vary your wording. Do make sure, though, that the meaning stays intact.

If you find yourself using the same word many times throughout your paper, get a thesaurus. Look up the word you are using and make note of similar words you could substitute. Replace this common word only with those that you would normally use, to avoid misusing the new words.

Does It Still Make Sense?

Throughout the editing process you replace words and phrases, take things out, and add other things. It is imperative that you keep rereading your paper to make sure it still makes sense after all of these changes. Editing is a process that uncovers flaws not only in spelling, grammar, and structure, but also in content.

ALERT!

Be sure that you use wording that is specific throughout your paper. If you continually make vague statements, it will be impossible for the reader to make a connection back to the paper's purpose. Every paragraph should be expressed clearly so that anyone who reads the paper understands your point.

Your paper still should include all the information that is necessary to understand the topic and your analysis of it. Check to make sure that the topic is clear to a reader who is unfamiliar with it. Include any essential information, but be sure that you don't include information that is irrelevant. It would be unusual to have to go back for more research at this point, but what you might find is that you cut out too much material during your previous editing.

Your paper should be developing a good flow and rhythm by this point. It should read like a polished and professional report rather than the rough, unedited version you began with. Ideas should flow from one sentence to the next, with smooth transitions between paragraphs. Any stories or timelines should be in order. As you read, you should never have to look back to recheck details, because your paper shouldn't jump from one section to the next or from one idea to the next. The main idea should always be clear, and it should always be evident that the paper is working toward a singular purpose.

From Thesis to Conclusion

As you proofread your paper, you need to ensure that it follows a specific path. Your research paper should begin with the thesis statement, present the research, and conclude with a statement that sums up how the research related to the thesis. There is always a purpose to the paper. It is sometimes easy to get so caught up in the research that you lose sight of the whole point of the paper. Don't let that happen. Proofread with an eye on how your paper goes from thesis to research and back to the conclusion of the thesis itself.

Stay Focused

Your research can be so fascinating to you that you lose sight of the focus of your topic. This is particularly true if you are researching a topic that you feel passionate about. You can find yourself drifting off the main path of your topic and getting lost in the details that are related, but not directly relevant, to your topic. As you proofread, make sure that you don't make the same mistake in your writing. Background information and supporting details are necessary, but resist the temptation to add something extraneous just because it is interesting.

Proof of Your Thesis

The paper should always point back to the thesis statement made at the beginning. At any point in the paper you should be able to see the relationship between the information being discussed and the thesis. You should not meander so far off topic that the reader would be confused about where the research is heading. The conclusion at the end of the paper needs to wrap up all the information that you presented, demonstrating how it relates back to the thesis. It should either answer a question or prove a point that the thesis began.

Use Active Voice

Use the active voice throughout all of your writing. It brings the paper to life, making it much stronger and more interesting. Your instructor may or may not have a preference for active voice, but most readers prefer it.

Though the passive voice is not wrong, it tends to make a paper boring to read. In many cases, passive voice is used to write sentences in the past tense. Once you bring the sentence into the present, you need to be change it into active voice. Notice that actions happen *to* the subject in passive voice, whereas the subject *performs* the action in active voice. For example, you could write "To prepare for the day she will take over, the motor home is being driven by Marley," but that is bland. If you turn it into the active voice and write "Marley drives the motor home herself to prepare for the day she takes over," the sentence becomes livelier.

Sometimes it doesn't make much sense to use active voice. An in-depth, scientific discussion may seem trivial if it is written in active voice, because that could take the emphasis off the main subject of the discussion. For example, when you state that "the boy was attacked by three large dogs," the emphasis is on the boy. If you changed that sentence into the active voice and stated "three large dogs attacked the boy," the emphasis is on the dogs. Some parts of your paper may be better in passive voice as long as the meaning isn't confused. Sometimes sentences using passive voice can end up too long, and sometimes using passive voice shifts the focus of a sentence. If this helps to focus the sentence on an area that you want to emphasize, it makes sense to use passive voice. In general, you should use the passive voice when you want to focus on the object that is receiving an action rather than on the subject that is performing the action.

Use Parents, Siblings, and Friends as Proofreaders

You can enlist the people you know to act as proofreaders. Ask your parents, your friends, your siblings, or your roommates if they will proofread your paper for you. You could offer to trade proofreading with someone in your class. Any of these people are likely to offer an opinion that is different from your own. They are a step further removed from the topic of your paper, which means they are reading the paper from a fresh perspective. Try to find people who are familiar with your topic as well as some who know nothing about your topic. That will give you some well-rounded feedback. Those familiar with your topic may spot errors in content or be able to tell you what important things you have left out. They may be able to give you some firsthand information or anecdotes that you can use in your paper. Don't forget to double-check their information just as you would any other source. Those who are new to your topic can tell you if you are skipping over too many details and leaving the reader confused.

A new set of eyes can often spot errors that you may have skipped over. Another proofreader can tell you which parts are confusing and which parts make sense, and can also pick out grammatical and spelling errors that you missed. When you read your own writing you will sometimes fail to see all these errors because you made them yourself.

Once you find people willing to proofread your paper, don't just give them red pens and let them get to work. You need to know exactly what errors they have marked, and you don't want to be left with a confusion of crossed-out lines and messy additions. Ideally, both you and your proofreaders should know the standard symbols that proofreaders use. Not only will this come in handy while they proofread your paper, but you will understand what the symbols mean when an instructor marks it. (You can find a list in *The Chicago Manual of Style,* as well as in dictionaries and other reference books.) If this isn't feasible, at least be very clear about what it is you want your proofreaders to do, and in what form you would like their feedback.

Re-Draft!

By this time your research paper is full of markings and edits. You may have rewritten parts of it. Now it is time to re-draft it. This could be a one-time process, or you may need to re-draft a few times before you are happy with it.

This is another good time to take a day away from your project. If you forget about it completely and clear your mind of any thoughts of your topic, you will be able to return with a fresh perspective. You might even return with some new ideas about how to improve your new draft. Words and phrasing that aren't quite right are more likely to jump out at you now. After some reflection, you may decide that some of the things you included in your first draft and later took out belong back in there. Put them back in if you truly think they belong, but be careful not to return everything to your paper and end up with your original first draft. If you had good reasons to edit the material out, you need even better reasons to put it back in.

QUESTION?

What if I didn't leave myself enough time to set it aside for a day?
You should be able to at least take a short break. Do something completely different that requires your concentration. Physical activity is a great break from writing research papers. Watching television, however, doesn't really get your mind to focus on anything intensely, and so isn't much help.

Read through your paper one more time. Try to identify any weak sentences or paragraphs and rework them until you are satisfied that they express exactly what you want to say. Any improvements are a good thing. Use more descriptive language, eliminate anything that is not direct or to the point, and clarify details. Carry on with this process until you believe that your draft is the best it can be.

Chapter 21

Adding Extra Touches

If you want your paper to really stand out, it is worth the effort to invest some time in adding extra touches. Whether it's a photograph, a chart, or a hand-drawn illustration, these extra elements bring your paper to life and help to illustrate what may be difficult to explain in words. Check with your instructor before you begin, because there are usually some guidelines to follow. Some instructors truly appreciate these additions, while others don't welcome them. Usually, though, you can't go wrong by putting in extra effort.

Making It Special

Adding nontext elements to your research paper can greatly enhance its presentation. While you probably have a well-thought-out paper at this point, these extra touches mark it as truly original and special. In some cases, these elements really aren't extra at all, but an integral part of your topic and the reader's understanding of it. Although the wording of your paper is of course the most important part, an above-average presentation improves its value.

The sources of any visual aids that you copy or cut out to use in your research paper must be included in your bibliography. Follow the instructions in Chapter 15 for citing sources.

Choosing Visual Aids

Extra touches include any and all visual aids that are applicable to your topic. Some readers have trouble visualizing what you are talking about unless they can actually see it. Visual aids are a way to bring your ideas to life. You don't need to be an artist to add visual touches to your project. Some visual aids can be photographed or created on a computer or cut straight out from the source. Some are charts or maps or other diagrams that don't require artistic skill.

Every image that you use in a research paper, whether maps or drawings or charts or something else, needs a title that describes exactly what is shown. Clearly label any other pertinent information, and assign a figure number to every image that is referenced in the text.

Visual aids also serve to break up what would otherwise be solid pages of words. Magazine publishers understand this very well and make ample use of photographs and other visual elements. Anyone can get tired of reading page after identical page. Graphic representations of your research add interest. For example, if your paper includes a large amount of statistical data, it will be very difficult to present as solid text. A graph or chart can show this data in a clear and arresting way that holds the reader's interest. Visual aids can either repeat information that is already included in the text of your paper or they can present data for the first time. Again, check with your instructor in case there are any specific rules about the types and numbers of visual aids that you can use. Before you put any effort into developing these extra touches, make sure you are permitted to use them.

Budget Your Time

Make sure that you don't spend too much time on visual effects. Though the extras are important, the research paper itself is of prime importance. In fact, if you don't have the time available, don't add any visual effects at all. These should be thought of as an extra component that, although a worthy addition to your paper, are not necessary. Only take the time to do them if you still have time left after the rest of the paper is complete. Choose the types of visual aids that you know you can present well and that are directly related to your topic. If your paper deals with the most obscure discoveries made by Alexander Graham Bell, a map of his childhood town would not contribute to the paper in any way. Drawings of some of his inventions would be ideal.

QUESTION?

How do I get a map to come out to scale when I draw it?
You can start by photocopying and reducing a large map to the size you need. Then trace the outline of the map, filling in only those details that are necessary. Now it is to scale, and you can add all of your own information and details.

Maps

Maps that are relevant to your topic demonstrate where things are in relation to each other, which aids the reader's understanding. There are different ways you can present maps. You can draw your own, either by hand or using a computer graphics program, or you can trace or photocopy an existing map. You need to specify in your paper which method you chose.

Accuracy

The method you choose will have some bearing on the accuracy of your map. If the map is drawn without any relationship to actual distances, you need to specify that it is "not to scale." If it is not to scale you should still make your best effort to put things as close as possible to their correct place. If a city should be right on the border of a state, don't place it somewhere near the middle. Maps are much more useful if distances are measured out and drawn appropriately. The area in question is then shown in perspective and relative locations can be determined. Obviously, maps that you trace or copy will already show these correct relationships.

All maps should include three specific elements: a scale showing how actual distances relate to the distances on your map, a north arrow so that people will know which direction they are looking at, and a legend showing the meanings of any coloring, shading, or symbols on your map.

Historical Maps

If you look hard enough, you usually can find historical maps that contain many different types of information. These are quite interesting and can add a lot to your paper if they apply to your topic. Historical maps are not just limited to showing places as they were at various points in the past; they also frequently show such varied things as economic activity, military troop movement, vegetation, traffic patterns, radio coverage, and recreation areas. Though you won't be able to add an original historical map to your paper, you can possibly redraw or even trace the map, depending on where you find it.

Specialty Maps

Just as there are many different types of maps for historical periods, there are even more types of modern-day maps. Advancing technology has created the ability to draw maps using satellite and infrared images. Because of these new capabilities, more types of maps are available now than ever before. Instead of searching through maps to find one that fits with your topic, decide what type of map you need first and then try to find it. If a library or museum doesn't have it, a map retailer can probably help you out. You can order specialty maps from online retailers such as Omni Resources (*www.omnimap.com*) or Maps.com (*www.maps.com*).

Most atlases contain more than just basic maps. Both historical and specialty maps of some description can be found in a regular atlas. You can also find many different specialty atlases, as explained in Chapter 5. Your search for a unique map shouldn't have to take you too far.

Adding Drawings

If you can draw reasonably well, you can illustrate something in your research paper. Depict people or places or events as they actually are, or as they were historically. Don't draw your own interpretation of what they might have been like. Remember that this is a formal research paper, not an informal novel.

Depending on any guidelines you were given, you may be free to use whatever drawing materials you wish on whatever type of paper you want. However, you should ensure that whatever you use is long-lasting and will not get smudged. If you are going to spend the time to create a drawing, you should also spend the time to ensure its durability.

Original Art

Hand drawings should be done using whatever medium you are most familiar with. Make sure that whatever you use is durable, and that any illustrations are labeled. It may seem obvious, but also be sure that any original art is the same size as your report. Don't use an extra-large sheet of paper and then try to add it to a standard-size research paper.

It is handy to be able to include a drawing whenever the actual picture is not available for your use, or if you want to use only a portion of a whole picture. For instance, you may find a photo of a group of kids skateboarding, but it is for a safety poster and doesn't reflect the skateboarders relevant to your topic. What you are trying to capture is the appearance of the skateboarders, including their age, their clothing, and the tricks they are performing. If you find another photo of kids who are dressed like the ones you want to illustrate, you can draw one skateboarder using the combined features you want to depict, without overwhelming the illustration.

Traced or Computer-Generated Art

Luckily, if you are less artistically inclined, you can either trace a drawing or photo or generate one using a computer. In this case, you may use all or part of someone else's illustration, so you need to cite your source correctly. Tracing is the quicker way to create an illustration, but the computer will give you much more flexibility. Software programs such as Adobe Photoshop and Adobe Illustrator are popular for this purpose. You can add color with one click of the mouse, or resize different parts of your drawing. You can rotate, outline, or add special effects. With both methods you can easily add or remove different components to suit your needs.

FACT

At some point you probably will come across clip art and wonder if you can use it in your research paper as is. Clip art is ready-to-use artwork available as a computer file. Some of it is free to use for student papers and some of it is not, so you need to check with the source of each file.

Photographs

Because a photograph is a true representation, it can illustrate facts in a way that no other visual aids can. Photos are also a fairly simple way to illustrate a research paper, because there is nothing you have to do to a photo before you use it in your paper.

You can find photos of some kind almost everywhere. Don't think of photos as only the ones you see in museums or the ones sent out by publicity campaigns. You can cut photos out of magazines and newspapers. You can download photos off the Internet. Postcards are just photos, as are calendar pictures. If you have the software and the skills, you can manipulate photographic images on your computer. You can add captions or crop certain portions of the photos. Even stock photos, which are professional photos that you can purchase for some purposes, are usually reasonably priced. Photos should always be cited in your bibliography. Professional photographers are usually fairly generous with requests to use their photos for school projects but even so you should never assume that all photos are for public use. Check to see if the photo has a copyright (it will usually state the copyright in small letters beside the photo) and if so, ask for permission before you use it.

QUESTION?

How do I use my own photos in a research paper?
You have a choice. You can either use the original photo and attach it securely to your paper, or you can scan the photo into a computer file (if it is not already a digital photo) and then insert it on the proper page.

Suppose you search every place you can think of and you still cannot find a photo that suits your purpose. If you have a digital camera or have enough time left for developing print film, consider taking the photos yourself. Obviously this will only work out for you in some cases, but it is an option that some students overlook. For example, you may decide to write a paper about potential nuclear disasters. You happen to live near the site of the Three Mile Island nuclear accident of 1979. You find one aerial photo of the nuclear power plant in a magazine, but you want to show how close it is to the neighboring communities. You'd like a photo taken from someone's front door looking toward the plant, or from the gates of the plant looking out toward some nearby housing. Because this is almost in your own neighborhood, there is nothing to stop you from taking those photos yourself.

Charts and Diagrams

Visual aids can also include any type of charts and diagrams. While these are considered to be visual images, they are simply a way of representing data in a graphic form. Many of your hard facts will become more interesting if they are presented in this way. These graphic forms are a simple way to display comparisons between different data or between different periods in time.

Choosing a Type

There are many different types of charts, diagrams, and graphs. Certain types are used more often in research papers. One of these is the *frequency polygon*. This is also referred to as a line chart. A frequency polygon is used to show comparisons over time between different items.

Another type is the *histogram*, also referred to as a *bar chart*. This also shows comparisons and can contain many different items. Performance is shown as a solid bar instead of the single line used for a frequency polygon.

Pie charts, which are the ones that most of us are most familiar with, show the proportion of parts to a whole. The parts are shown as percentages.

The *pictograph* is not commonly used in research papers. This chart is so named because it includes a picture in the form of a drawing to further illustrate what is being compared. The picture is generally shown on a bar chart.

If you need to illustrate the steps that are taken to perform a certain task or to carry out a sequence of events, you might want to use a *flow chart*. This depicts each step and where it falls in the process. For example, you could use a flow chart to show the steps you should take to write a research paper.

A *column chart* is very similar to a bar chart, but it is usually used to show two or more different items at specific stages. It could also show comparisons between these items.

To show how different tasks, events, or ideas compare, use a *Venn diagram*. A Venn diagram usually shows three separate tasks that overlap which illustrates what these tasks have in common and how they differ.

Use a *cycle diagram* when you want to show a process that is part of an ongoing cycle. These are commonly used to display life cycles. There are various steps along the process, but they all return back to the beginning, where the cycle starts again.

A final commonly used diagram is the *pyramid diagram*. This is used to represent data that builds on a foundation. Typically, the top of the pyramid represents something more desirable than the bottom. (You are probably familiar with the food pyramid from grade school, which illustrates the basic food groups and how much of each type we should eat.)

When to Use Them

Charts and diagrams are ideal when you have large amounts of data to convey. Instead of simply listing all the data, you can show it visually. This allows readers to see relationships and processes where before they saw only numbers and information. Often the biggest question is not whether to use charts and diagrams, but which type to use. There are usually only one or two types that will best fit the information you need to convey. It may take some experience to figure out which type of visual aid works best for which type of data. Any of these charts and diagrams can be included on a page of text. Avoid splitting any of these types of figures into two parts. If you cannot fit the entire figure on the page you began it on, see if you can place it elsewhere in the paper. It may even need a page of its own.

Creating a Web Site

You could choose to set up a Web site for your research paper. This is a method of self-publishing your paper, and it allows you to share the information you found with the rest of the world. Include the URL of your Web site somewhere in your paper so that your instructor can refer to it. You should only create a Web site if you have solid knowledge about how to do so. Otherwise, you will find yourself spending far too much time on this one small aspect of your paper.

If you decide to go ahead with a Web site, determine what you want to include. Will you publish your entire research paper on this site? Will you just post a summary and highlights of your research? Will you post only your raw notes? This is really your own decision. There is no right or wrong way to do this; just make sure that everything is in your own words. If you include notes from a personal interview or from any other person-to-person contact, you should first let that individual know that his or her words will be posted online.

A few specific things should be omitted from this Web site. You need to be especially careful if you publish your entire paper on the site. Remove personal contact information from the cover page and any other places within your paper. This includes not only your own personal contact information but also that of any sources or other people you mentioned. Remove all personal phone numbers, student identification numbers, and home addresses.

Designing a Cover Page

When you wrote reports back in elementary school, you paid a lot of attention to creating cover pages that were visual masterpieces. You used lots of color, covering almost the entire page with illustrations both large and small. Your title was in large, multicolored balloon-style letters. Now you have moved past that. A cover page is still required, but it will be much more formal this time around.

You have to include specific information on a cover page. This is fairly standard no matter where you are attending classes. The cover page usually includes the title of the research paper, your full name, information about the type of paper that it is, the course you are writing it for, and the date it is submitted. That is actually all that is required. You may use a small graphic to liven it up a bit if you present it in a neat and polished manner. A black-and-white graphic, whether a drawing or photo or map, looks more professional than does a color graphic. A background image could be larger and incorporate some color, but remember that an image should not be the focal point of the cover page.

You may be told not to include a cover page. In fact, many style guidelines, such as MLA style, indicate that you should not have one. Still, most instructors do seem to like them. If your paper does not include a cover page, the information you would have put on that page must appear somewhere else, probably on the first page of your paper. The information should be double-spaced in the top left-hand corner. There is no need for any extra lines in between your own name, the title of your paper, the course you are writing it for, and the submission date. Leave two or three blank lines after this information to set it off from the text of your paper.

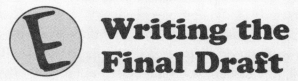

Chapter 22

Writing the Final Draft

It is ironic that the only part of the research paper that people will see, the part that looks as though it took a lot of work, is actually the easiest part of the entire process. From your viewpoint, all of the work is already done. All that is left for you to do is to present the paper in the proper format, making sure that it is neat and clean. Your first draft and all the subsequent revised drafts come together in this one final draft.

Neatness Counts

The content of your paper reigns supreme, but neatness always makes a better impression. In some ways, handing in a research paper is no different from going to a job interview. The outcome should be dependent on what you say, but that first impression can make a real impact. Make sure that your paper looks crisp and clean and professional.

You may be tempted to rush through the final draft. After all, by this point you have been working on your research paper for weeks. Because you are so close to being finished, you might just want to get it done and out of the way at all costs. Resist this urge to rush. It takes time to produce a neat copy. This is true whether you are typing the paper or writing it by hand. Leave yourself plenty of time to finish the paper and to reread it in case you want to make some last-minute changes. If you scheduled your time well, you planned to have the final draft completed a few days before the due date. Assuming nothing has gone wrong and you are still on time, you now are able to read and reread this draft until you are positive there are no errors.

If you find mistakes on your final draft, you can use correction fluid in a neat manner. Pages with more than two corrections should be rewritten or retyped. Some instructors may let you have as many as three corrections per page.

Check your final draft for any errors in typing. If you write your paper using a word processing program, you will of course check it before you print it. Because your final draft is the result of revisions made directly to your earlier drafts, you are less likely to find these sorts of errors than if you were writing your paper by hand. However, mistakes do still happen, so verify that there are no errors before printing. If you find an error in your printed paper, make the correction and reprint the page. Some students find it difficult to spot errors on a computer screen. If that's true for you, print your draft before you check it for errors.

If your paper is handwritten, you will have to look at other options. Correction fluid comes in many different forms, and if it is used correctly it doesn't affect the neatness of your paper. If it is used incorrectly it tends to blotch and smear, leaving your paper a mess. You can use the liquid form or the tape or the pens, whichever is easiest for you. They are nearly invisible. However, if you end up with a lot of corrections on one page, it is better to rewrite the page. A paper covered in correction fluid looks like the work of an amateur. Never make corrections by crossing out a word or by writing over a word or letter. These always look messy.

Instructor Requirements

Despite the fact that most research papers have similar requirements, some instructors have their own preferences. You should always check with your instructor or with any guidelines you were given before you assume that you can use a normal format. If your instructor has no preference, you should use the generally accepted standards as explained here.

Formatting

Use only white, letter-size paper—that is, 8½ x 11 inches. You should type or write on only one side of this paper. Each side of the page, and the top and bottom, should have a one-inch margin. Most word processing programs will default to this margin anyway, but you will need to remember it yourself if you are writing your paper by hand. The reasoning behind this is twofold. The margin adds to the visual appeal of the paper, and it gives the instructor room to write comments about your work.

Usually paragraphs will be indented; however, this is an area where your instructor may differ. Some prefer to see all the text aligned to the left margin with an extra space between paragraphs to set them off.

All research papers should be double-spaced. Again, this is both for visual appeal and for your instructor's comments.

Number your pages and include your last name in case the papers come apart and get mixed up, either within your own report or with others'. The page number and last name should always appear in the top right-hand corner of each page, aligned to the right and top margins. So, for example,

Spalding 1, Spalding 2, Spalding 3, and so on, should appear in the top right-hand corner of consecutive pages. Some word processing programs include a function to automatically add the page numbers to each page. You can customize this function to show your last name as well.

If your paper includes headings for separate sections, make sure that these are clear. They often stand out better if they are in bold type and if they include an extra blank line before and after the heading. Never switch to a different font for a heading. The style guide you are using should specify how to treat headings; in any case, make sure they are consistent throughout.

Type your paper in a regular font such as Times New Roman or Arial. A font size of 12 is the easiest to read. If you write your paper by hand, use black or blue ink, never any other colors, and never pencil.

FACT

Most instructors like to follow the presentation guidelines in the *MLA Handbook*. There are specific instructions for margin widths, paper size, spacing, page numbering, and citation requirements. Some of your instructor's requirements may vary slightly from these guidelines, so don't just assume that you can follow them all.

How a research paper should be bound together is still a matter of some debate. The only consensus seems to be that a paper should be bound. Some people just staple or clip the pages together. Others like to use report covers or binders, though some instructors discourage those. If they are allowed, be sure to pick one that fits the papers as closely as possible, not one that is oversized or bulky. Avoid anything overly fancy; it will only detract from the otherwise professional presentation of your paper.

Organizing Your Paper

Make sure that the pages of your paper are in the correct order before you hand the paper in. You numbered your pages, so this should be easy. If you are handing in other components of your research, perhaps because your instructor has asked to see your first draft, he or she might ask you to include these items at a certain place in your paper or to hand them in separately. You are always required to include the bibliography, and it is always placed at the very end of the research paper. Make sure that your drawings, maps, figures, and photos are in the appropriate spot in your paper, and that the cover sheet is at the beginning.

Using a Computer

Most students use a computer to write their research papers. Occasionally, an instructor will ask for a handwritten paper just to make sure that students are doing their own work and are not losing the ability to work neatly without the help of a computer. However, this generally applies only to very young students. Your instructor is likely to require a typed paper, but just in case, it may be helpful to review the pros and cons of each.

Advantages

The computer does have many advantages over writing papers by hand. Obviously, computers are used in more and more facets of our lives all the time, so computer skills are becoming much more important. Typewritten pages look neat and clean, and errors can easily be fixed. You can set up formatting so that all pages have identical margins and headers. Although their effectiveness is limited, grammar and spell checkers can help find some errors that you might miss. You will also find computers to be advantageous when you are revising your initial drafts. Not only can you move words and phrases within your document; using multiple windows, you also can easily switch back and forth between one document and another. For example, you could have your draft report, bibliography, and notes all open at the same time. Finally, with a computer you don't have a stack of papers to deal with until you are ready to print the final draft.

Disadvantages

The biggest downside of writing your research paper on the computer is not knowing how to type, or not having adequate typing skills. Typing is considerably quicker than is writing by hand, but only if you know how to type. It is not a difficult skill to learn, however. You can use one of the easy tutorials on the Internet (for example, Learn2Type at *www.learn2type.com*) or an inexpensive software program (for example, *Mavis Beacon Teaches Typing*) to learn how to type. Even if you don't have time to learn before your current assignment is due, consider learning in the near future, because this is a skill you will need throughout school and beyond.

The other possible disadvantage to using a computer is not having one at your disposal at all times. Even if you have a computer at home, you may not have access to it when you need it if you share it with other family members.

Word Processing Programs

You can use a wide range of programs to type your research paper on a computer. They vary greatly in terms of cost, ease of use, and features. While you may just choose to use what is available to you on the computer that you have access to, you might also want to make some decisions about which program would best suit your needs. There is no need for any program that performs more functions than you will ever use. Choose the program that suits your particular requirements for now and into the foreseeable future.

Notepad and SimpleText

Programs like Notepad and SimpleText are basic text editors. They are free and usually come with any new computer. These text editors are very simple, and it doesn't take much time at all to learn how to use them. Another advantage is that they allow you to copy files into other programs without the problems you will encounter trying to do this with some of the more powerful programs. The main disadvantage of a basic text editor is that it doesn't offer any frills. There are no spell checkers, no special text fonts, and no other formatting capabilities such as automatic pagination or outlining features. If you don't need any of these capabilities, these programs are a good choice.

MSWorks and ClarisWorks

MSWorks, ClarisWorks, and similar programs contain word processing as part of a multifunctional package. They generally also have spreadsheet capabilities and a database, and some contain more functions as well. These programs sometimes are included free with a computer, but they also are available for a reasonable cost. The word processing function offers more features than a text editor does, but it still is not as robust as a full-fledged word processing program.

Microsoft Word and WordPerfect

MicrosoftWord and WordPerfect are two of the most popular programs specifically designed for word processing. They enable extensive formatting, with features such as spell and grammar check, outlining functions, bulleted lists, tables, and more. They also allow you to add graphics to a document. Their main drawback is cost. While some computers are sold with one of these word processing programs already installed on them, others aren't, and these more sophisticated programs run into the hundreds of dollars. Though their features are impressive, you may not really require them.

Adobe PageMaker and QuarkXPress

PageMaker and QuarkXPress are powerful desktop publishing programs that add visual impact to the pages you create. These programs, which often are used to produce brochures, cards, and signs, are very powerful and versatile. They also are very expensive and probably beyond what most people will ever require for their personal use.

Report Covers and Binders

Your research paper needs to be held together in some fashion. Your instructor will tell you whether report covers and binders are permitted at all, and if they are, whether there are any restrictions. If you are allowed to use them, make sure you don't choose one that detracts from your project.

A report cover can convey some aspect of your personality or your topic, but it should not take your individuality to extremes. Your research paper needs to look professional, not cute. Stay away from fluorescent colors or anything with more than just a subtle design on it. If a cover is not one that would be appropriate in a professional work setting, it is also not appropriate for a research paper.

There are many different types of covers and binders. Sometimes you need to punch two or three holes in the paper you use to get it to fit in a particular binder, but you can find binders that don't require holes. Shop around when you are looking for a report binder; there are many kinds to choose from. Although you want to present your paper in a dignified, professional manner, you can still express some degree of individuality.

Avoiding Overkill

One mistake students make is to focus too hard on the presentation of their paper. They tend to get carried away with making it look nice and end up being excessive. There is a distinct difference between a professional presentation and an excessive presentation, and you should strive to find a balance between the two.

The focus of your paper needs to be on the paper itself. You should not put more effort into the way the paper looks than you did into what the paper contains. It should be clean and tidy. Though there is room for some embellishments, keep them to a minimum.

ALERT!

Even the best presentation can't make up for a lack of content in your paper. If you are feeling at this point that you need to add extra touches to your paper because it can't stand on its own merits, you need to take the time to revisit the paper itself and correct any flaws it contains.

There are some things that instructors definitely frown upon. We've all heard the stories about students who handed in papers on scented notepaper or who included food or even cash in the hopes of eliciting a good grade. While most students wouldn't even consider going to those extremes, you may be tempted to do some less obvious things. Although your paper will stand out if you use a different color or type of paper, it won't be for the right reasons.

Nothing should accompany the paper other than the required elements. Avoid attaching a personal note to the instructor, which will only make it seem as if you don't believe the paper is good enough to stand on its own. Hand in what is required, and only what is required.

A final but vital thing to avoid is handing the paper in late. You know the due date and you know to whom the paper should be given, so there is no excuse for a late assignment.

Presenting Your Research Orally

In some instances, you will be asked to also give an oral presentation of your research paper. This is an opportunity to display how much you have learned about your topic. You can also take this opportunity to add any arguments that support your stance on an issue that you discuss in your paper. There is no reason to dread an oral presentation. It is really an occasion to expand on what you talked about in your research paper.

Know the Requirements

Make sure you understand exactly what you are being asked to do. Are you being asked to read your entire paper, or should you summarize it? Will you present to people who have already read your paper? What are the minimum and maximum time limits? Know how many people you will present to, and where you will give the presentation. Find out the level of formality that is required. Will you present to a group of peers or to a panel of academics? The more you know about your presentation ahead of time, the easier it will be to prepare an appropriate talk.

You should also know when you will make your oral presentation. You should know the exact date and even the time of day for your presentation.

Know Your Presentation

As you prepare for an oral presentation, you need to practice repeatedly. Don't memorize your speech word for word, but know the key points you want to cover. If you have been given a time limit, cover all the vital information in that period of time. Run through the information you want to relay a few times to make sure that you are within the right time range. If you know your presentation well, you are more likely to be able to maintain eye contact with your audience and to speak clearly so everyone will know what you are saying. Both are qualities of a good speech.

Just as you wrote the introductory paragraph of your research paper with the goal of capturing the reader's attention, you now will state your introduction with the goal of capturing the listener's attention. Begin with a startling fact that you learned from your research, or a strong opinion that you want to convince the listeners to agree with.

Use Visual Aids

If you are allowed to use them, visual aids provide a boost to your oral presentation. Used correctly, they enable the audience to use the sense of sight as well as hearing, so they have a better chance of fully understanding what you are talking about. Visual aids can include any sort of prop that is related to your topic, including maps, charts, overhead projections, and slides. Practice with these visual aids prior to your presentation. You need to make sure that everything is working properly and that you have everything you need, including extension cords and pointers. If you need to use special equipment, such as an overhead projector or a slide projector, arrange for that with your instructor ahead of time. You also want to ensure that any of these visual aids can be seen clearly from anywhere in the room.

How do I make overheads more legible?
You should use large, uppercase letters in any labels or other writing you use. All overheads should be as simple and as uncluttered as possible. Don't use any yellow coloring, because it won't show up on the projection. Finally, a few good overheads are preferable to a lot of mediocre ones.

Calming Your Nerves

Some people are at ease with making oral presentations, while others get very nervous. Nervousness can cause shaky hands, pauses in the speech, and a voice that is hard to hear. Avoiding these presentations isn't a solution, because you will have to do more of them throughout your life. Take preemptive action to calm your nerves so that you can excel at the presentation.

Practice is probably the best thing you can do to help calm nerves. Speeches get easier every time you do them. You already know all aspects of your topic because of your research. You can pick one or two people in the crowd, at opposite sides of the room, and pretend you are speaking just to them.

Publishing Your Research

Now that you have worked so hard to produce this paper, you are probably quite proud of it. It represents not only many long hours of research work, but it also highlights your own analysis and discovery about your topic. It makes sense, then, to show your paper to your peers. You can accomplish this by having it published.

Why Publish?

All students of upper-level classes should be encouraged to publish their research, for a number of reasons. You compiled information from a number of different sources. Then you added your own analysis and ideas, which makes it advantageous to others to share what you've learned with them. Publishing is also advantageous to you. It exposes your work to further assessment. It allows your paper to be judged to ensure that it is of the standard that it should be. Publishing your research paper is an important step toward getting a job in the academic field of your choice. Once you have published a paper in that field, your name will begin to be noticed.

Where to Publish

If getting your research paper published is important to you, it is just as important to get it published in the right place. There are three places where you are likely to get your paper into print. The first possibility is to publish your work on a Web site, either on your own site or on an existing site. This is the option open to most research papers at the high school level and some at the college level. The downside to this option is that such Web sites are not as well-respected within the academic community as are the printed journals.

The best place to pursue publication for an upper-college-level research paper is a peer-reviewed journal. Be sure to identify the journals that are appropriate for your topic. If you try to get published in a journal that is not closely related to your topic, not only will your paper be turned down, it will not be read by the people you are trying to reach. The journals with more prestige are those run by professionals in their discipline. The largest of these might have a circulation of up to 3,000, but the smaller ones are focused on more specialized topics.

You are probably already aware of what the relevant journals are. You quite possibly already read them, or you may have used them as a research source. To find others, look in Ulrich's Periodicals Directory at ✐ *www. ulrichsweb.com/ulrichsweb/* or the ISI Master Journal List at ✐ *www.isinet. com/journals/.* You can also find both of these in book form at your library.

How to Publish

There is a two-step process to follow to get your research paper published. First, check the instructions to authors for the journal or journals you have selected. These are guidelines that deal with layout, style, and the submission process itself. Second, send your paper to the editors. They will forward it to a committee or review board for consideration. The more prestigious the journals, the larger the committee. These individuals will judge your paper for its appropriateness, completeness, and accuracy. This process can take months and even up to a year or more. Some newer Web-only journals that publish much sooner are beginning to develop, but of course they do not have the same respect as the offline journals.

Chapter 23

Real-Life Research Papers

You've now completed what was quite possibly the most intense assignment you have done to date. A well-done research paper is a real accomplishment. But you may be wondering how this will ever translate into something you will use away from school. This wasn't just an exercise to fulfill a course requirement. Learning how to write a research paper has taught you vital skills that will serve you well in both your working life and in your day-to-day life at home.

When Will You Ever Use These Skills?

You have probably already had experiences in which you could have used research paper skills. It is unlikely that you would have made the connection between what you were trying to discover and the exact skills you needed. Even now you may not understand how writing a research paper will ever help you in other circumstances. If you review the process, however, you may begin to appreciate just how much you accomplished.

Skills You Learned

You learned and/or perfected a number of new skills. Though you may have had prior knowledge in some areas, others were completely new to you. To begin with, you learned how to narrow your options to one specific choice when you selected a topic. This decision-making process dealt with brainstorming and prioritizing. Then you moved on to scheduling. There you learned how to arrange your available time in order to complete a task. In doing so you had to set priorities, deal with setbacks, and allow for other commitments.

As you began to look for data and information, you increased your research skills incrementally, looking up information in volumes that you didn't even know existed and uncovering new possibilities for places and methods to conduct research. You learned how to find what you need at a library and when to approach the librarian for assistance. As you looked through various sources, including magazines and newspapers, movies and radio, museums and city hall, you found out about the wide variety of information that is ready to use if you know where to look.

Throughout the research process you may have uncovered sources that were not reputable. Some may have had incorrect information, and some may have been misleading. In addition, you learned how to determine the integrity of your sources, and you became adept at taking notes from source information and rewriting it your own words.

Quite possibly you conducted an interview or two. You were responsible for setting up the interview, deciding what direction the interview would take, and pulling information from that interview.

Once you gathered all this information, you learned how to properly cite every source that you used. Following this you organized all the information you found and created a logical procedure for presenting that information. You added in your own analysis of the data or your own arguments to support your opinion of the information. You were able to turn all of this into an organized paper that included an introductory paragraph, the body of the paper, and a concluding paragraph.

Before your project was complete you learned to be a fact checker, a proofreader, and an editor. You used some graphic representations of the topic, and you may have presented your paper orally. That is quite a collection of skills to learn from one assignment.

ALERT!

Obviously, one other thing you gained from this process is an in-depth knowledge of the topic you chose. By performing this research you learned much more about the topic than you ever would have by listening to an instructor. You also were able to develop your own perceptions about the topic based on what you found.

Real-Life Applications

Will you ever use these skills in real life? Actually, you are already using them, even if it isn't apparent to you. These are not just skills that aid you whenever you do another research paper; they are skills that will help with a lot of your other schoolwork as well. These skills also will come in handy in your future jobs or careers, and they will be of assistance at other points in your life outside of work and school. You will build on the basics you learned every time you put one of these skills to use again.

Even the skills that are not directly related to research can easily be used in other situations. For example, you learned how to conduct an interview. This will help you even if you are the interviewee in the future. At a job interview, you will be able to see how the interviewer is trying to lead you in a certain direction. You will understand that the interviewer is looking for explanations, not just brief answers.

You also learned organizational skills. The skills you developed by creating an outline can be utilized in many other areas of your life as well. You know now how to arrange things in a logical order and how to purge things that are unnecessary. Whether you decide to chair a committee, start a business, or organize a fundraiser, organizational skills will be a crucial aspect of your efforts.

You gained valuable experience in writing paragraphs properly, which will be very useful if you are ever in a situation in which you need to do a lot of writing. This is a learned skill, not just something that people can automatically do well. It will benefit any other subjects you study, almost all of which require writing skills, and it will also improve your personal writing.

Personal time management is a skill that many people would like to develop further. You had to schedule your time and rearrange that schedule at points throughout the research process, and you can apply those same techniques to your daily life. You learned how to estimate the amount of time it will take you to complete a task and found out whether those estimates were realistic. Even if you made mistakes, the errors provided valuable information for future tasks you undertake, in school or out of school.

Day-to-Day Examples

The most personal ways you will put these skills to work are in segments of your day-to-day life. We all conduct mini research projects of our own all the time without being aware of it. Every time we look for more information about something, or we make comparisons between two or more things, we are conducting a research project to some extent. You use research skills on a regular basis—every time you make a purchase or decide how you feel about an issue or make a decision about your future. Now that you have developed those skills even further, you can make even more informed choices.

Researching Colleges

A college search is a prime example of a personal research project. You start out with a purpose; in this case, finding the college that is the best fit for your needs. You need the information by a certain date, similar to the due date for your paper. Your primary method of gathering information is requesting information from the various colleges that you are interested in. You then evaluate that information and make comparisons based on the courses available, the location of the college, the size of the college, the tuition fees, residence availability, and perhaps extracurricular activities. You may have other needs or interests on which you would base your comparisons. You might find some people who have attended these colleges, and talk to them about their impressions. This is your more informal version of an interview.

Once you narrow down the field to a few choices, you may visit some of these colleges. In doing this you are undertaking even more focused research. You may look at college rankings, both academically and in the other areas that you feel are important. You need to judge this information for accuracy and dependability. As you wrote your paper you learned to look closely at all information and question its reliability, and this is a perfect real-world application of those skills.

QUESTION?

Are there other ways to apply these skills in daily life?

It is not just the research skills that you will use again. From this process you learned to discern between good information and questionable information; you learned writing skills that will help in any communications task; and you learned how to read and understand charts or graphs as you created the ones you used in your paper.

Making Purchases

Whether you are buying a bottle of vitamins, a flashlight, a truck, or a house, you research the product first. For example, before you go grocery shopping you do research by looking through the refrigerator and cupboards to see what you need to buy. You may go online to see what recipes you can prepare from the ingredients you have on hand. If you look through the fliers that come in the mail to see which stores have the foods you need on sale, you are again doing research. Even in the grocery store, you may carefully read labels to check sodium or sugar content, comparing two or more brands.

If you are about to make a large purchase, such as a truck, you go through a similar research process, but it is on a larger scale. You gather research by walking through car lots and looking at the cars. You may test-drive some of them. While you are there you talk to a sales associate and maybe pick up a brochure or two. You might read through some books and magazines about trucks, paying particular attention to the features of the new models. At some point you may read a book or an article that compares different makes and models. Some other possible sources for your research are auto shows, truck-related Web sites, and of course the opinions of people around you.

You can see that a lot of the research you undertake for personal reasons involves the same kind of research and analysis that you did for your paper, but without the presentation. You are not likely to write up a report on your findings for the examples just described, although you might if you write an advice column or do research for work.

Work-Life Examples

In your working life you will probably take these skills one step further. Depending on the type of job you have, you may actually end up writing reports that are very similar to research papers. You may also make oral presentations to your colleagues, superiors, or customers. It will be a great benefit to you if you can do them well. Effective communication skills can mean the difference between getting a job, retaining a job, or getting a promotion.

FACT

In a workplace research project, you may find yourself working as part of a team. Each team member is given one distinct task to carry out. Then they collaborate on the end results. While this gives each person less control over the project, many unique ideas contribute to the result.

Analyzing Data

In almost any career you will be called upon to make comparisons between different products, different processes, or different services. Let's say you are a plumber. On any given job you might be comparing products or suppliers or even new plumbing technology. You will use a lot of the knowledge you already have about the products, but you would probably also talk to other plumbers or salespeople and you would read documentation about plumbing products. Because you would be considering using these products, suppliers, or technology, you would be continuously evaluating and analyzing them.

If instead you were an environmental engineer, you might be working with facts and data. You might take water samples from a lake, for example, and have them tested for various impurities to determine the lake's sources of pollution. You would probably provide a lot of visual information based on your findings. The results from the test could be shown on a histogram that would display the various test locations and what level of each impurity was found there. You could also use a pie chart that could show which locations contained the greatest percentages of impurities. Interviews with local citizens could round out your research. In this case you would probably present both a written report and an oral presentation. You would still follow all the steps you went through to produce a research paper.

Lobbying Effectively

Your job may also involve lobbying for change of some kind. Then you would quite possibly go through a process similar to the one you did when writing a persuasive research paper. Suppose you work for an ophthalmology clinic. At this clinic many eye surgeries are performed, but one new technique can reduce or eliminate vision problems in older adults. The problem is that the cost of this surgery is not subsidized at all for many patients. You would like to see that changed, because you have seen some ideal candidates for the surgery who couldn't afford to have it done. You gather some case study material from the clinic's patients, get details about the surgery from the ophthalmologist you work for, and begin to write what really amounts to a research paper. You pay close attention to fact checking because this is such a technical topic. Then you take your paper to the appropriate governing body and present it at one of their open meetings. Because you know how to organize and present your research well, your project is carefully considered and begins to bring about a change in policy.

Making a Living as a Researcher

Although you will find yourself using segments of your research knowledge in many different careers, some jobs focus almost completely on research. If you enjoyed digging for facts in as many different places as you could think of, these could be fields that would interest you, because they would allow you to use most of the skills you learned while doing your research paper. If you can find work that combines your skills with what you enjoy doing, the weeks you spent on your research paper will be time well spent.

Library Jobs

You must have noticed when you asked the reference librarian for help that he was an expert at finding information in all sorts of obscure places. He could pull out reference books that you had never heard of, and he knew how to track down information that wasn't available in that particular library. He knew all that because his entire job is based on performing research, classifying materials, and helping library users find specific information. There are other jobs in a library as well, especially in a larger library. Most libraries that are big enough have a different librarian for each specialized area, such as films and videos or magazines and newspapers. Each of those library employees is proficient at performing research work in a particular area.

FACT

According to statistics from the American Library Association, reference librarians across the country answer more than 7 million questions every week. These include librarians working in public libraries as well as those working in academic libraries. This association also found that more than 95 percent of the nation's public libraries have Internet access available to the public.

Reporter/Journalist

Reporters and journalists work for television, radio, newspapers, and magazines. Their job is to research hot topics or interesting new developments or timely events. They are continually working through the research process. The result of their research will be a written presentation or an oral presentation, but generally not both. Reporters and journalists almost always spend a lot of their research time conducting interviews. They learn to be experts in picking out the best people to interview and in getting the most detailed or controversial information out of that person. Unfortunately, they never have weeks to complete one assignment, so they don't get to dig as deeply into a topic as you did in your research paper. However, because they are often dealing with topics that are at the forefront of the news, not a lot of background information needs to be researched. Most readers or listeners or viewers would already have a basic knowledge of the topic.

You will need an advanced degree if you want to pursue most careers in research. Interestingly, you will write many more research papers while you are working toward that degree. Pay close attention to those papers, because with each one you will further develop your skills.

Other Research Careers

There is almost no end to the variety of research careers you could go into. Every branch of science conducts its own research, and scientists working in those fields go through a process very similar to writing a research paper. These careers include the following small sample:

- Agricultural research
- Pharmaceutical research
- Animal behavior research
- Research analysts
- Social research
- Market research
- Meteorological research
- Biospace research
- Web researcher

Web Researcher

The last item on the preceding list, Web researcher, is a relatively new career field. Employers now are looking for people who are proficient at finding information on the Internet. This is not just someone who knows how to look something up with a search engine, but someone who can think creatively and knows what other methods to use to access information. Web researchers usually work for someone who needs a lot of research done but doesn't have the time to sort through the seemingly endless information available, separating the good from the bad. The skills you gained in finding a variety of research sources and in evaluating these sources are applicable here.

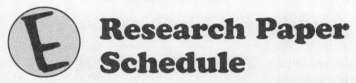

Appendix A

Research Paper Schedule

Use this schedule template to plan the time you need to complete your research paper. Start by filling in today's date at the top and the final due date at the bottom. Use the schedule guidelines explained in Chapter 4 if you are unsure how long each step should take. Be sure to allow for additional assignments and other commitments. Fill in the target date for each task, and then refer back to this schedule as you work through your project.

Today's Date

Choose the Topic

Task	Proposed Completion Date
Research:	
Encyclopedias and Reference Material	
Books	
Periodicals	
The Internet	
Films, Videos, Sound Recordings	
Television (check dates and scheduling)	
Radio (check dates and scheduling)	
Movies (check dates and scheduling)	
Museums and Historical Sites	
City Hall	
Set Up and Prepare for Interview	
Conduct Interview (date and time of appointment)	
Create the Outline	
Write the First Draft	
Proofread, Edit, and Check Facts	
Maps, Drawings, Photos, Charts, and Cover Page	
Write the Final Draft	
Prepare Oral Presentation	
Due Date	

Appendix B

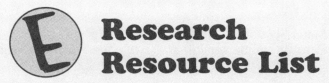

Research Resource List

Y ou are likely to find many worthwhile resources as you work your way through your research paper. It's a good idea to bookmark or otherwise keep a list of the best resources you find as you visit the library and search the Internet. This list of the most relevant sources for research is a good starting place.

Encyclopedias

Encyclopaedia Britannica

32-volume print set as well as an online version at *www.britannica.com*

World Book Encyclopedia

22-volume print set as well as an online version at *www.worldbookonline.com*

Almanacs

The World Almanac and Book of Facts

More than 1,000 pages, including news stories, maps, and flags, as well as information about education, health, nations of the world, the economy, awards, and more

The World Factbook

Published every year with maps and country profiles and histories. Updates are at the related Web site at *www.cia.gov/cia/publications/factbook/*

Dictionaries

Merriam-Webster's Collegiate Dictionary

Contains more than 215,000 definitions

Dictionary of American Slang

Contains more than 19,000 slang terms

Roget's Superthesaurus

Contains more than 300,000 synonyms

Atlases

National Geographic Atlas of the World

More than just maps, this also includes illustrated articles and country flags and facts

The Great Atlas of the Stars

Shows constellations, mainly those best seen from the Northern Hemisphere

Atlas of World History

Maps from different points in history

Archives

U.S. National Archives & Records Administration

✑www.archives.gov

Library and Archives Canada

✑www.collectionscanada.ca

The National Archives of England, Wales, and the United Kingdom

✑www.nationalarchives.gov.uk

Smithsonian Institution

✑www.si.edu

Other Web Sites of Interest

Society Hill Directory of Historical Societies

Genealogical and Historical Societies in the United States, Canada, and Australia

www.daddezio.com/society/index.html

ProfNet Global

Access to professional sources that caters to reporters. There is a cost for this, but some colleges and universities have access to it.

www2.profnet.com

Online Article Archive

Search and read articles from more than 900 publications

www.findarticles.com

Our Documents

100 milestone documents of American history

www.ourdocuments.gov

Repositories of Primary Sources

Large listing of sources for research

www.uidaho.edu/special-collections/Other.Repositories.html

Inter-University Consortium for Political and Social Research

Archive of data from research projects

www.icpsr.umich.edu

Appendix C

Glossary

These terms, some of which are unique to research papers, relate to the areas of research, writing, proofreading, and presentation.

Active voice

The voice in a sentence that shows that the subject of the verb is performing the action.

Annotated bibliography

A bibliography that includes a commentary about the works being cited.

Bibliography

A list of materials that were used to research a topic.

Bookmark

A browser function that enables a Web site to be marked for easy retrieval.

Call number

An alphanumeric combination used to organize books on library shelves.

Card catalog

A system for looking up all materials in a library, now usually computerized.

Citation

A standard format for listing all research sources.

Database

An organized collection of data.

Dissertation

A formal written composition that puts forward a new point of view based on research work that has been completed. A dissertation is usually required to obtain an advanced degree.

Interviewee

The person who is being interviewed.

Journal

An academic publication similar to a magazine.

Keyword

A word used to search the Internet or library catalog for relevant information.

Microfiche

Reproduction of texts placed on a flat sheet of film and read on a special machine.

Microfilm

Reproduction of texts placed on a strip of film and read on a special machine.

Passive voice

The voice in a sentence that shows that the subject of the verb is receiving the action.

Peer review

A process by which experts in a specific field assess a paper for suitability and accuracy.

Periodical

A magazine, newspaper, journal, or newsletter that is published on a regular basis.

Plagiarism

Using the information, writings, or ideas of another as one's own.

Primary source

The original source of information, such as an eyewitness account, letter, speech, or statistical data.

Public domain

Works that are freely available for use by the general public.

Quotation

An expression, either written or verbal, that is used in its exact original form.

Referee

The experts who review a paper as part of the peer review process.

Reference

A source used in research, commonly understood to include encyclopedias, dictionaries, atlases, and the like.

Search engine

A program on the Internet that enables a user to look for specific information.

Secondary source

Works that are not the original source of information, but are based on primary sources and add to them.

Term paper

A research paper that usually takes most of a term to complete.

Thesis

The main statement that a research paper sets out to prove.

Web Portal

A Web site that provides a wide range of resources for further exploration.

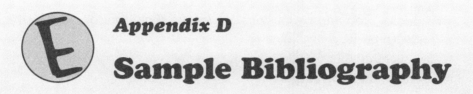

Appendix D

Sample Bibliography

Your bibliography will follow the format explained in Chapter 15. It should end up looking similar to the sample bibliography below. All sources cited in this sample are imaginary, but they follow the MLA citation style commonly used for research papers. The type of source is listed here in bold type above each citation. This labeling would not be present in your bibliography but is presented here for clarity.

Book by one author

Young, George. *Athleticism and Self-Esteem*. 2nd edition. New York, NY: Mulberry Press, Inc., 1999.

Book by two authors

Fredricks, Fred and Laura Wilst. *All for the Team*. Detroit, MI: Hoover, Inc., 2000.

Book by more than two authors

Mitchell, Rachel et al. *We Feel Good About Ourselves*. 4th edition. Chicago, IL: Applewood Press, 2004.

Magazine article

Spence, Paul E. "It All Starts Here." *National Educator* February 2001: 15–19.

Journal article

Dodd, Sheldon. "Natural Talent or Learned Enthusiasm?" *Sociology Today* 11.9 (2000): 89–93.

Newspaper article

Dreland, Mae. "To Be a Jock: Long Term Implications" *Freemarket News* 12 May 2003: B6.

Encyclopedia article

Ross, Emmett. "Kinesthiology." *The Real Encyclopedia*. 2nd edition. 12 vols. New York, NY: Clement Press, 1996. 9:768.

Web site citation

Norman, Hugh. "The Best Reason To Get Involved." My Time 04 Dec 2002. http://mytime.com/articles/involved.htm

Newsgroup posting

wuntowun. "not feeling optimistic." Online posting. 21 Jan 1999. 14 May 2004. <rec.people.general>

E-mail message

Yung, Joy. "Injury report." E-mail to Hank Lester. 31 Oct 2003.

Forum discussion

Chester, J. "Fitness Outcomes." Online posting. 11 Nov 2000. My Time Forum. 23 Sep 2001 <http://forums.mytime.com/messages=19.7>

Listserver discussion

Abbot, Jim. "Re: What do you think." Online posting. 09 Mar 1998. Special Ed. 30 Apr 1998 <list@specialed.com>

Movie

Final Game. Dir. Len Gordon. Perfs. Wanda Lee, Brett Guiness, Shelly Hartling. DVD. Jewel Pictures, 1997.

Personal interview

James, Flora. In-person interview. 02 July 2002.

Photo

Stewart, Floyd. "Boys Outside Mill Woods School." Apr 1933. Photographs from the Springdale Museum & Archives. [http://springdaleweb.net/photo/1428468] (25 Oct 2003).

Index

THE **EVERYTHING** SERIES!

BUSINESS & PERSONAL FINANCE

Everything® Budgeting Book
Everything® Business Planning Book
Everything® Coaching and Mentoring Book
Everything® Fundraising Book
Everything® Get Out of Debt Book
Everything® Grant Writing Book
Everything® Home-Based Business Book
Everything® Homebuying Book, 2nd Ed.
Everything® Homeselling Book, 2nd Ed.
Everything® Investing Book, 2nd Ed.
Everything® Landlording Book
Everything® Leadership Book
Everything® Managing People Book
Everything® Negotiating Book
Everything® Online Business Book
Everything® Personal Finance Book
Everything® Personal Finance in Your 20s and 30s Book
Everything® Project Management Book
Everything® Real Estate Investing Book
Everything® Robert's Rules Book, $7.95
Everything® Selling Book
Everything® Start Your Own Business Book
Everything® Wills & Estate Planning Book

COOKING

Everything® Barbecue Cookbook
Everything® Bartender's Book, $9.95
Everything® Chinese Cookbook
Everything® Cocktail Parties and Drinks Book
Everything® College Cookbook
Everything® Cookbook
Everything® Cooking for Two Cookbook
Everything® Diabetes Cookbook
Everything® Easy Gourmet Cookbook
Everything® Fondue Cookbook
Everything® Gluten-Free Cookbook

Everything® Grilling Cookbook
Everything® Healthy Meals in Minutes Cookbook
Everything® Holiday Cookbook
Everything® Indian Cookbook
Everything® Italian Cookbook
Everything® Low-Carb Cookbook
Everything® Low-Fat High-Flavor Cookbook
Everything® Low-Salt Cookbook
Everything® Meals for a Month Cookbook
Everything® Mediterranean Cookbook
Everything® Mexican Cookbook
Everything® One-Pot Cookbook
Everything® Pasta Cookbook
Everything® Quick Meals Cookbook
Everything® Slow Cooker Cookbook
Everything® Slow Cooking for a Crowd Cookbook
Everything® Soup Cookbook
Everything® Thai Cookbook
Everything® Vegetarian Cookbook
Everything® Wine Book, 2nd Ed.

CRAFT SERIES

Everything® Crafts—Baby Scrapbooking
Everything® Crafts—Bead Your Own Jewelry
Everything® Crafts—Create Your Own Greeting Cards
Everything® Crafts—Easy Projects
Everything® Crafts—Polymer Clay for Beginners
Everything® Crafts—Rubber Stamping Made Easy
Everything® Crafts—Wedding Decorations and Keepsakes

HEALTH

Everything® Alzheimer's Book
Everything® Diabetes Book
Everything® Health Guide to Controlling Anxiety

Everything® Hypnosis Book
Everything® Low Cholesterol Book
Everything® Massage Book
Everything® Menopause Book
Everything® Nutrition Book
Everything® Reflexology Book
Everything® Stress Management Book

HISTORY

Everything® American Government Book
Everything® American History Book
Everything® Civil War Book
Everything® Irish History & Heritage Book
Everything® Middle East Book

HOBBIES & GAMES

Everything® Blackjack Strategy Book
Everything® Brain Strain Book, $9.95
Everything® Bridge Book
Everything® Candlemaking Book
Everything® Card Games Book
Everything® Card Tricks Book, $9.95
Everything® Cartooning Book
Everything® Casino Gambling Book, 2nd Ed.
Everything® Chess Basics Book
Everything® Craps Strategy Book
Everything® Crossword and Puzzle Book
Everything® Crossword Challenge Book
Everything® Cryptograms Book, $9.95
Everything® Digital Photography Book
Everything® Drawing Book
Everything® Easy Crosswords Book
Everything® Family Tree Book, 2nd Ed.
Everything® Games Book, 2nd Ed.
Everything® Knitting Book
Everything® Knots Book
Everything® Photography Book
Everything® Poker Strategy Book
Everything® Pool & Billiards Book
Everything® Quilting Book
Everything® Scrapbooking Book

All Everything® books are priced at $12.95 or $14.95, unless otherwise stated. Prices subject to change without notice.

Everything® Sewing Book
Everything® Test Your IQ Book, $9.95
Everything® Travel Crosswords Book, $9.95
Everything® Woodworking Book
Everything® Word Games Challenge Book
Everything® Word Search Book

HOME IMPROVEMENT

Everything® Feng Shui Book
Everything® Feng Shui Decluttering Book,
    $9.95
Everything® Fix-It Book
Everything® Homebuilding Book
Everything® Lawn Care Book
Everything® Organize Your Home Book

EVERYTHING® *KIDS'* BOOKS

All titles are $6.95

Everything® Kids' Animal Puzzle & Activity
    Book
Everything® Kids' Baseball Book, 3rd Ed.
Everything® Kids' Bible Trivia Book
Everything® Kids' Bugs Book
Everything® Kids' Christmas Puzzle
    & Activity Book
Everything® Kids' Cookbook
Everything® Kids' Crazy Puzzles Book
Everything® Kids' Dinosaurs Book
Everything® Kids' Gross Jokes Book
Everything® Kids' Gross Puzzle and
    Activity Book
Everything® Kids' Halloween Puzzle
    & Activity Book
Everything® Kids' Hidden Pictures Book
Everything® Kids' Joke Book
Everything® Kids' Knock Knock Book
Everything® Kids' Math Puzzles Book
Everything® Kids' Mazes Book
Everything® Kids' Money Book
Everything® Kids' Nature Book
Everything® Kids' Puzzle Book
Everything® Kids' Riddles & Brain Teasers Book
Everything® Kids' Science Experiments Book
Everything® Kids' Sharks Book
Everything® Kids' Soccer Book
Everything® Kids' Travel Activity Book

KIDS' STORY BOOKS

Everything® Fairy Tales Book

LANGUAGE

Everything® Conversational Japanese Book
    (with CD), $19.95
Everything® French Phrase Book, $9.95
Everything® French Verb Book, $9.95
Everything® Inglés Book
Everything® Learning French Book
Everything® Learning German Book
Everything® Learning Italian Book
Everything® Learning Latin Book
Everything® Learning Spanish Book
Everything® Sign Language Book
Everything® Spanish Grammar Book
Everything® Spanish Practice Book
    (with CD), $19.95
Everything® Spanish Phrase Book, $9.95
Everything® Spanish Verb Book, $9.95

MUSIC

Everything® Drums Book (with CD), $19.95
Everything® Guitar Book
Everything® Home Recording Book
Everything® Playing Piano and Keyboards
    Book
Everything® Reading Music Book (with CD),
    $19.95
Everything® Rock & Blues Guitar Book
    (with CD), $19.95
Everything® Songwriting Book

NEW AGE

Everything® Astrology Book, 2nd Ed.
Everything® Dreams Book, 2nd Ed.
Everything® Ghost Book
Everything® Love Signs Book, $9.95
Everything® Numerology Book
Everything® Paganism Book
Everything® Palmistry Book
Everything® Psychic Book
Everything® Reiki Book
Everything® Tarot Book
Everything® Wicca and Witchcraft Book

PARENTING

Everything® Baby Names Book
Everything® Baby Shower Book
Everything® Baby's First Food Book
Everything® Baby's First Year Book
Everything® Birthing Book
Everything® Breastfeeding Book
Everything® Father-to-Be Book
Everything® Father's First Year Book
Everything® Get Ready for Baby Book
Everything® Get Your Baby to Sleep Book,
    $9.95
Everything® Getting Pregnant Book
Everything® Homeschooling Book
Everything® Mother's First Year Book
Everything® Parent's Guide to Children
    and Divorce
Everything® Parent's Guide to Children
    with ADD/ADHD
Everything® Parent's Guide to Children
    with Asperger's Syndrome
Everything® Parent's Guide to Children
    with Autism
Everything® Parent's Guide to Children with
    Bipolar Disorder
Everything® Parent's Guide to Children
    with Dyslexia
Everything® Parent's Guide to Positive
    Discipline
Everything® Parent's Guide to Raising a
    Successful Child
Everything® Parent's Guide to Tantrums
Everything® Parent's Guide to the Overweight
    Child
Everything® Parent's Guide to the Strong-
    Willed Child
Everything® Parenting a Teenager Book
Everything® Potty Training Book, $9.95
Everything® Pregnancy Book, 2nd Ed.
Everything® Pregnancy Fitness Book
Everything® Pregnancy Nutrition Book
Everything® Pregnancy Organizer, $15.00
Everything® Toddler Book
Everything® Tween Book
Everything® Twins, Triplets, and More Book

All Everything® books are priced at $12.95 or $14.95, unless otherwise stated. Prices subject to change without notice.

PETS

Everything® Cat Book
Everything® Dachshund Book
Everything® Dog Book
Everything® Dog Health Book
Everything® Dog Training and Tricks Book
Everything® German Shepherd Book
Everything® Golden Retriever Book
Everything® Horse Book
Everything® Horseback Riding Book
Everything® Labrador Retriever Book
Everything® Poodle Book
Everything® Pug Book
Everything® Puppy Book
Everything® Rottweiler Book
Everything® Small Dogs Book
Everything® Tropical Fish Book
Everything® Yorkshire Terrier Book

REFERENCE

Everything® Car Care Book
Everything® Classical Mythology Book
Everything® Computer Book
Everything® Divorce Book
Everything® Einstein Book
Everything® Etiquette Book, 2nd Ed.
Everything® Inventions and Patents Book
Everything® Mafia Book
Everything® Philosophy Book
Everything® Psychology Book
Everything® Shakespeare Book

RELIGION

Everything® Angels Book
Everything® Bible Book
Everything® Buddhism Book
Everything® Catholicism Book
Everything® Christianity Book
Everything® Jewish History & Heritage Book
Everything® Judaism Book
Everything® Koran Book
Everything® Prayer Book
Everything® Saints Book

Everything® Torah Book
Everything® Understanding Islam Book
Everything® World's Religions Book
Everything® Zen Book

SCHOOL & CAREERS

Everything® Alternative Careers Book
Everything® College Survival Book, 2nd Ed.
Everything® Cover Letter Book, 2nd Ed.
Everything® Get-a-Job Book
Everything® Guide to Starting and Running
    a Restaurant
Everything® Job Interview Book
Everything® New Teacher Book
Everything® Online Job Search Book
Everything® Paying for College Book
Everything® Practice Interview Book
Everything® Resume Book, 2nd Ed.
Everything® Study Book

SELF-HELP

Everything® Dating Book, 2nd Ed.
Everything® Great Sex Book
Everything® Kama Sutra Book
Everything® Self-Esteem Book

SPORTS & FITNESS

Everything® Fishing Book
Everything® Golf Instruction Book
Everything® Pilates Book
Everything® Running Book
Everything® Total Fitness Book
Everything® Weight Training Book
Everything® Yoga Book

TRAVEL

Everything® Family Guide to Hawaii
Everything® Family Guide to Las Vegas,
    2nd Ed.
Everything® Family Guide to New York City,
    2nd Ed.
Everything® Family Guide to RV Travel &
    Campgrounds

Everything® Family Guide to the Walt Disney
    World Resort®, Universal Studios®,
    and Greater Orlando, 4th Ed.
Everything® Family Guide to Cruise Vacations
Everything® Family Guide to the Caribbean
Everything® Family Guide to Washington
    D.C., 2nd Ed.
Everything® Guide to New England
Everything® Travel Guide to the Disneyland
    Resort®, California Adventure®,
    Universal Studios®, and the
    Anaheim Area

WEDDINGS

Everything® Bachelorette Party Book, $9.95
Everything® Bridesmaid Book, $9.95
Everything® Elopement Book, $9.95
Everything® Father of the Bride Book, $9.95
Everything® Groom Book, $9.95
Everything® Mother of the Bride Book, $9.95
Everything® Outdoor Wedding Book
Everything® Wedding Book, 3rd Ed.
Everything® Wedding Checklist, $9.95
Everything® Wedding Etiquette Book, $9.95
Everything® Wedding Organizer, $15.00
Everything® Wedding Shower Book, $9.95
Everything® Wedding Vows Book, $9.95
Everything® Weddings on a Budget Book,
    $9.95

WRITING

Everything® Creative Writing Book
Everything® Get Published Book
Everything® Grammar and Style Book
Everything® Guide to Writing a Book Proposal
Everything® Guide to Writing a Novel
Everything® Guide to Writing Children's Books
Everything® Guide to Writing Research Papers
Everything® Screenwriting Book
Everything® Writing Poetry Book
Everything® Writing Well Book

Available wherever books are sold!
To order, call 800-258-0929, or visit us at **www.everything.com**
Everything® and everything.com® are registered trademarks of F+W Publications, Inc.